AF854506

The Essential 401(k) & IRA Retirement Guide

What to Do With Your Retirement Accounts Before and After You Retire

Susan Delaney

Table of Contents

Disclaimer

This book is intended for educational and informational purposes only and does not constitute financial, investment, tax, or legal advice. The information provided is based on general principles and publicly available sources as of the time of writing and may not reflect the most current laws, regulations, or individual circumstances.

Retirement accounts, tax rules, and financial strategies can vary widely based on personal factors such as income, age, employment status, location, and changes in legislation. Before making any financial decisions, including those involving 401(k) plans, IRAs, investments, withdrawals, or tax strategies, readers should consult with a qualified financial advisor, tax professional, or legal professional who can assess their specific situation.

The author and publisher make no guarantees regarding financial outcomes and disclaim any liability for loss, damage, or adverse results arising directly or indirectly from the use or application of the information contained in this book. Past performance of investments or strategies discussed does not guarantee future results.

By reading this book, you acknowledge and agree that you are solely responsible for your financial decisions and outcomes.

Copyright

Copyright © 2026 by Susan Delaney
All rights reserved.

No part of this book may be reproduced, stored in a retrieval system, or transmitted in any form or by any means, electronic, mechanical, photocopying, recording, or otherwise, without the prior written permission of the publisher, except as permitted by applicable copyright laws (Fair Use).

For information, contact:
Susan Delaney
publishing@essentialretirementguide.com

This book is intended for informational purposes only. The advice and strategies contained herein may not be suitable for every individual, and the author and publisher disclaim any liability or responsibility for any loss or damage resulting from the use of this material.
While every effort has been made to ensure the accuracy of the information provided, the author and publisher make no representations or warranties regarding the completeness, accuracy, or applicability of the content to your particular situation.

eBook ISBN: 979-13-992704-1-9

Paperback ISBN: 979-13-992704-0-2

Hardback ISBN: 979-13-992704-6-4

First published 01/2026.
Printed and bound in the United States.

A Message to the Reader

If you're reading this, retirement is no longer an abstract idea.

Maybe it's five years away.
Maybe it's next year.
Or maybe you're already there—wondering if you've made the right choices.

At this stage of life, the questions feel heavier:

Will my money last?
Am I paying more in taxes than I should?
What happens when I start taking money out?
Did I miss something important?

If any of those thoughts have crossed your mind, take a breath.

You don't need perfect timing, advanced financial knowledge, or risky strategies.
You need **clear information, calm decision-making, and a plan that fits your life**.

This book was written for people exactly where you are—people who want to protect what they've built and enjoy the years ahead without constant financial anxiety.

Let's start by making sense of what you already have.

Why This Book Exists

Most retirement books focus on saving more or investing aggressively.

But many people nearing retirement don't need more complexity—they need clarity.

This book exists to help you:

- Understand your 401(k) and IRAs in plain language
- Avoid costly withdrawal and tax mistakes
- Make confident decisions without fear or guesswork

Every chapter is designed to help you move forward—one clear step at a time.

Other Books in The Essential Retirement Strategy Series

Practical guides designed to help you make smarter retirement decisions and build long-term financial security.

Available Now

The Essential 401(k) & IRA Retirement Guide

Learn how retirement accounts work, how to maximize contributions, and how to create a smarter withdrawal strategy for long-term financial stability.

The Essential Social Security Retirement Guide

How to maximize your benefits, avoid costly claiming mistakes, and coordinate Social Security with your retirement plan.

The Essential Retirement Tax Strategy Guide

How to reduce taxes on retirement income and build a tax-efficient withdrawal strategy.

The Essential Retirement Income Blueprint

How to turn retirement savings into reliable income streams that last throughout retirement.

Coming Soon

The Essential Medicare Planning Guide

How to select the right Medicare plan for you and protect yourself from unexpected medical expenses.

The Essential Early Retirement Blueprint

Learn how to build a realistic strategy to retire early and learn how to make you money last.

Introduction

Most people don't think seriously about retirement until it stops being theoretical — usually somewhere in their thirties or forties, when a number on a 401(k) statement starts to feel like it actually matters. By then, a lot of people also feel behind: nearly half of American workers have less than $25,000 saved for retirement, and it's easy to read a statistic like that and assume everyone else already figured this out while you missed the memo.

You didn't miss anything. Retirement planning isn't confusing because you failed to learn it — it's confusing because almost nobody is taught it. Your employer hands you an enrollment form, points at a percentage box, and assumes you'll sort out the rest on your own. Multiply that by a few decades of acronyms — IRA, RMD, SECURE 2.0 — and conflicting advice from every direction, and "I should already know this" stops being a fair thing to think about yourself.

This book exists to close that gap. It covers what a 401(k) and an IRA actually are, how the employer match works, what taxes do to your money under each account type, and the handful of decisions — timing, contribution percentage, what to do when you change jobs — that matter more than most people realize. Social Security helps, but it was never designed to cover a full income on its own; the accounts in this book are what's meant to fill that gap.

Two things you can count on from here: I won't use a term without explaining it, and you won't get scolded for where you're starting from. Whether you're opening your first 401(k) or trying to make sense of accounts you've had for fifteen years, the explanations ahead assume you're capable, not behind.

Let's start with Chapter 1.

Chapter 1: Meet Your Retirement MVPs: 401(k)s and IRAs Unveiled

Chapter at a Glance

What you´ ll learn in this chapter:

- What a 401(k) and an IRA actually are — and how each one shelters your money from taxes while it grows
- Why the employer match is the single best deal in personal finance, and how to make sure you're capturing all of it
- The difference between pre-tax and after-tax contributions — and why it matters more than most people realize
- Three myths that stop people from saving — and the truth that makes each one easy to dismiss

Estimated reading time: 25 minutes

> **FIELD NOTE** *I've talked to people in their sixties who had been contributing to a 401(k) for twenty years and still weren't sure how it worked. That's not embarrassing — it's the norm. This chapter fixes that. By the time you finish it, you'll know more about these accounts than the majority of people who use them every day.*

'Most people don't learn how retirement accounts work until they're already supposed to have one. Nobody teaches it in school. Your employer hands you a form, points to a percentage box, and expects you to figure the rest out on your lunch break. This chapter fixes that. Many wonder if it's too early to begin, too late to catch up, or whether their paycheck is even enough to make a difference. These questions are common, and the answers might surprise you. This chapter invites you to explore straightforward ideas that can help turn confusion into confidence, showing how everyday choices today quietly shape the comfort and freedom of tomorrow.

Retirement Account Essentials: 401(k)s and IRAs Explained

Imagine starting a new job and learning you have a 401(k) plan waiting for you, like a special plot in the company's community garden. You get to plant your financial seeds here and watch them grow with help from your employer. With a 401(k), you decide to put part of your paycheck into a retirement account before taxes get taken out, which means you pay less in taxes now. For example, if you earn $3,000 a month and put $300 into your 401(k), your taxable income for that paycheck shows up as $2,700 instead. This not only helps lower what you owe in taxes today, but it also leaves more of your money to keep working for you inside your retirement account, like planting extra seeds that will sprout in the years ahead.

A big reason people love 401(k) plans is the employer match. When your boss decides to match your contributions, it is almost like receiving free money for your garden. If your company matches up to 3% of your salary, and you put in 3%, they will match you dollar for dollar. So if you make $50,000 a year and contribute $1,500, you get another $1,500 from your employer. This is a gift that can significantly boost your savings over time. IRS contribution limits for 401(k) plans are adjusted periodically, so the exact dollar amount can change from year to year. Before making contribution decisions, check the current annual employee deferral limit and any catch-up contribution amount on IRS.gov.[5].

The magic of a 401(k) is not just in the free money or the tax savings today. It also grows without being touched by taxes year after year. Suppose you invest in stocks or mutual funds inside your 401(k), and your investments earn more over time. You do not pay taxes on those earnings each year. Instead, your whole harvest gets to grow, undisturbed, until you retire and start using the savings. Think of it like letting your garden flourish season after season before you ever pick any vegetables. When you finally begin withdrawals in retirement, you will pay regular income tax on what you take out, but by then, you may be in a lower tax bracket and have a bigger harvest.

While 401(k)s are garden plots provided by employers, IRAs are more like buying your own patch of soil, wherever you want. Anyone with earned income can open an Individual Retirement Account, whether you work full-time, part-time, or freelance. You get to choose the location and care for your investments your way. Unlike a 401(k), IRAs are not tied to any employer; you can start one through a bank, a brokerage, or a mutual fund company. This appeals to those who want control or who do not have access to an employer's plan.

There are two main types of IRAs—Traditional and Roth. A traditional IRA may allow you to deduct some or all of your contribution, depending on your income, filing status, and whether you or your spouse is covered by a workplace retirement plan. Your investment then grows tax-deferred, just like in a 401(k), and you pay taxes only when you eventually start withdrawing money, usually after age 59½. For example, if you put in $6,000, and it grows to $30,000 over decades, you owe no taxes on the growth until you make withdrawals. A Roth IRA works differently: you pay taxes on the dollars you contribute now, planting already-taxed seeds. The upshot is that qualified Roth IRA withdrawals can be tax-free in retirement. In general, that means the account must satisfy the 5-year rule and the distribution must occur after age 59½, disability, death, or a qualified first-home purchase, subject to IRS rules.[5].

There are some important boundaries. 'You can contribute up to $7,000 annually to an IRA in 2025 ($8,000 if you are age 50 or older). These limits are set by the IRS and subject to annual adjustment, so always verify the current year limit at IRS.gov before contributing. Certain income limits may apply to Roth IRAs, making them off-limits to high earners, while Traditional IRAs have their own deduction rules. Employer matches are not part of the IRA world, since these plans are not linked to jobs. Instead, you have greater freedom choosing what to invest in—stocks, bonds, mutual funds, and more—allowing you to plant whatever you like in your personal patch.

Comparing a 401(k) and an IRA side by side helps clarify what suits different people. If you work at a company, the 401(k) offers a big patch of land with help from your boss, higher contribution limits, and sometimes a loan option if you need money temporarily. An IRA is the personal route, providing flexibility and a wider range of choices, which is great for people who want more control or have jobs without benefits. Both types help your savings grow beyond what would be possible in a regular account, thanks to the power of tax advantages and compounding growth.

Retirement accounts do more than store money. They build the safety net that supports dreams of travel, time with family, and freedom from anxiety about running short. Instead of only counting on social security, these accounts help create a future you can shape, making them the foundation for long-term financial security ([4]; [5]).

Motivation and Myths: Why Retirement Planning Matters More Than You Think

The math here rewards one thing above all else: starting. Not the amount, not the strategy — just the act of starting now instead of "eventually." It's easy to look at retirement saving as something distant—almost theoretical at first—but the returns from these accounts are very real and can shape your later years in ways both big and small.

Leaving retirement saving for "future you" can be as unwise as setting out on a sunny hike with no sunscreen. Things might seem fine at first, but the long-term consequences are painfully clear. Retirement accounts like 401(k)s and IRAs give your money a special place to grow, shielded from unnecessary taxation, with the advantage of compound interest quietly doing much of the heavy lifting. Every dollar you save is not just sitting still; it's working—earning interest and using that interest to earn even more, year after year ([1]; [6]).

People often hesitate to start, though, held back by some familiar beliefs. First, there's the classic, "I'm too young to worry about retirement." For a lot of twenty-somethings, the next weekend seems more pressing than the next thirty years. But youth gives you time, and time is the most powerful tool you can wield in the fight for financial security. Picture this: if a 25-year-old puts away just $100 a month in a retirement account and lets those savings collect a steady 7% annual return, that person could see their modest contributions blossom into well over $225,000 by age 65. Meanwhile, a friend who waits until 35 to start, putting in even three times as much money per month for half the years, may end up with a much smaller nest egg. Compound interest rewards early and steady saving, not just the size of your paycheck or your financial "muscle" later on ([1]; [6]).

Next comes the hesitation of the late starter: "It's too late for me." Life sneaks up, expenses pile on, and suddenly it seems like the window has closed. The truth is far more forgiving. While starting early is best, beginning to save later still brings meaningful rewards. For example, even someone saving just $250 a month between ages 50 and 65—assuming average returns—could still build a savings cushion of greater than $70,000. This may not buy a villa in the south of France, but it certainly makes the difference between a strained and a secure retirement. The key is consistency. Showing up every month for fifteen years beats one enthusiastic burst followed by silence.

Finally, there's the myth that saving is only for big earners: "I don't make enough to start saving for retirement." This misconception can be paralyzing, especially for anyone juggling bills, rent, or student loans. But take heart: even small, regular contributions harness the magic of growth over decades. Imagine setting aside only $25 a week. That's less than the cost of a few takeout lunches. Piled up over the course of a year, that's over $1,200. Over 40 years, with steady returns, even these small sums can multiply many times over, offering meaningful support in retirement [1]. Moreover, employer-sponsored plans regularly include contribution matches. That's free money, just for showing up and tending your plot—even if your earnings feel modest to begin with.

Retirement planning may seem mysterious, but in reality, it's simply giving yourself the best chance to relax later, whether that means lounging by a real pool or enjoying pancakes at your favorite diner. Regular saving is like applying financial sunscreen—you're quietly protecting yourself from future discomfort by doing something simple and smart today. Relying solely on Social Security is like going camping with only half a tent: it'll provide some shelter, but you'll probably want something sturdier. These accounts fill the gaps, ensuring that when work days are done, your lifestyle can keep on rolling [6].

Building financial security isn't about heroic leaps. It's about small, patient steps, taken day after day. Looking ahead isn't something to fear—it's like drawing up blueprints for a cozy home you'll enjoy for years. And the earlier you grab your watering can and start, the more chance you'll have to watch your financial landscape flourish, free from the regrets of inaction. Unpacking the tools and habits for proactive planning, and understanding the risks of waiting, only brings you closer to putting down stronger roots for tomorrow.

Proactive Planning: The True Cost of Waiting and How to Take Action

Strolling along the path to financial security, some employees view retirement accounts like dusty treasures in the attic—vaguely important but easily ignored. Yet, these accounts hold the key to a stable future. Neglecting to act early with 401(k)s or IRAs doesn't just mean missing out; it means actively shrinking the possibilities for a comfortable retirement. Imagine two co-workers: Alex, who starts saving at 25, and Jordan, who puts it off until 35. Even if Jordan eventually matches Alex's annual savings, the magic of compounding is no longer an ally. Every year Alex's early savings are working, multiplying without any extra effort. By the time both reach 65, Alex's account could be nearly twice as large—simply because she started sooner and let her money grow.

Procrastination in retirement planning isn't the same as forgetting to tidy up a closet only to get to it next week. Instead, delaying by just a few years can mean chasing after what's become a moving target. This happens because of a natural bias known as "future self neglect"—we find it hard to prioritize tasks that only produce visible rewards far down the road [2]. Many young employees rationalize, "I'll save more when I get a raise" or "I'll figure it out next year." Too often, next year turns into next decade. Stress mounts as retirement grows closer and the time window for catching up shrinks.

Picture the missed opportunities: small contributions left unmade, employer matches skipped, years of tax-free compounding lost. It's the classic last-minute rush scenario. Just as students panic-cram before an exam, late starters often scramble to sock away bigger chunks of their paycheck in their final working years—sometimes doubling or tripling their savings rate overnight. This is stressful, risky, and often impossible to truly make up for lost time [3]. Regret over retirement savings is surprisingly common, especially among older adults who wish they had acted sooner.

Many people hold onto a common myth—that Social Security will be enough to cover all or most expenses in retirement. In truth, Social Security is not intended to be most people's only source of retirement income. On average, it replaces about 40% of a worker's pre-retirement earnings, although the percentage varies by earnings history and claiming age. Because Social Security typically replaces only part of pre-retirement income, relying on it alone can leave a significant gap that personal savings may need to fill. [2]. Building up a dedicated reserve in 401(k)s or IRAs provides a crucial safety net against these uncertainties.

Choosing to let employer defaults dictate your retirement path is a bit like showing up every day to a cafeteria where the chef decides your meal—usually picking the plainest, least costly dish. It's easy to just say yes to these defaults, but a closer look reveals why that can be a big financial setback. Many employer retirement plans enroll workers at a minimum contribution—sometimes just 3% of pay—and invest the money conservatively. For a brand-new hire in their twenties, this can mean decades of missed growth. Making no changes to the default is comfortable, but rarely optimal [2]. Active participation—bumping up contributions every year, seeking out smarter investments—can mean the difference between settling for the basics and creating a truly secure nest egg.

Simple behavioral nudges can help: some plans now include a "Save More Tomorrow" option that lets employees pledge in advance to automatically raise their savings when they get a pay raise [3]. This small promise helps overcome procrastination and inertia by making future action easy—and research shows it can boost long-term savings rates dramatically.

Consider Lisa, who sets her retirement contributions at $200 per month at age 25. Compound interest does most of her work—by age 65, she could have nearly $400,000, assuming a modest annual return. Mark, starting at 35 with the same monthly amount, only amasses about $200,000 by retirement. The message is clear: time multiplies savings. Even modest, steady deposits into a 401(k) or IRA can grow into a solid cushion, making it less stressful to keep up with goals as life and expenses evolve.

Vivid mental images can help beginners. Picture a snowball at the top of a hill: the sooner it begins rolling, the larger and faster it grows. Early, regular contributions gain momentum, making every future dollar more powerful. Starting as early as possible means lighter lifting later on and far more peace of mind. For anyone, regardless of career stage, the best step is to move from passive to proactive—choosing higher savings rates, reviewing investments, and taking thoughtful ownership of their retirement journey ([2]; [3]).

The Bottom Line

Now that we understand the basics of 401(k)s and IRAs—their unique benefits, how they grow over time, and why starting early matters—we can take confident steps toward building a stable financial future. Whatever you start with – $25 a week or $250 a month – the amount matters less than the fact that it's happening automatically, every month, without you having to decide again each time. Demystifying these accounts shows us that saving doesn't have to be complicated or intimidating; it's about making simple choices that accumulate powerfully over time. With this foundation, you're ready to explore how to make the most of your money each day and shape a financial plan that grows with you, turning long-term goals into achievable realities.

As you move forward, remember that small, consistent steps matter far more than perfection. You'll also find a free toolkit to help you apply these ideas—details at the end of the book.

KEY TAKEAWAYS

- A 401(k) is tied to your employer. Contributions come out of your paycheck before tax, reducing your taxable income today. Your money then grows tax-deferred until you withdraw it in retirement.
- An IRA is independent – you open it yourself, regardless of where you work. Traditional IRAs offer a potential tax deduction now; Roth IRAs offer tax-free withdrawals later.
- The employer match is free money with one condition: you have to show up for it. Always contribute at least enough to capture 100% of whatever your employer offers.
- Starting early matters more than the amount. A 25-year-old saving $100 a month will, in most scenarios, retire with more than a 35-year-old saving $300 a month – because time is doing the heavy lifting.
- No income level is too low to benefit. Even $25 a week adds up to over $1,200 a year, and over four decades of compounding, that changes the picture considerably.

Next up: How compound interest actually works – and the one number that explains why starting now always beats starting later.

Chapter 2: How Money Grows: The Magic of Compound Interest

Chapter at a Glance

What you´ ll learn in this chapter:

- What compound interest is, how it differs from simple interest, and why the gap between them widens dramatically over time
- The Rule of 72: a quick mental calculation that tells you how fast your money will double at any given rate of return
- A side-by-side look at what starting at 22 versus 32 actually costs you in real dollars
- A step-by-step exercise so you can run your own numbers and see your potential growth

Estimated reading time: 20 minutes

> **FIELD NOTE** *The math in this chapter isn't designed to impress you — it's designed to change how you see time. Most people underestimate what ten years of compounding is worth. Once you see it on paper, it tends to stick.*

There is a number that changed everything about how people think about retirement savings — and it is not a dollar amount. It is time. Specifically, it is the difference between starting at 25 and starting at 35. That gap, which feels small when you're living it, is where fortunes are made or missed. Let's look at exactly why. They miss how time and patience play a crucial role, and they don't realize what happens when interest starts earning interest on itself. This growing, compounding effect can feel mysterious or even like magic, but it's really about simple steps that build upon each other over time.

This chapter explores that quiet force behind growth—the way money can multiply under the right conditions—and why when you start matters just as much as how much you save. Through everyday examples and easy exercises, you'll see how small contributions become significant, how waiting affects what you might lose, and how understanding these ideas can help anyone take control of their financial future without feeling overwhelmed.

The Foundations of Compound Interest and the Power of Starting Early

Money has a way of growing in your savings account, but the way it multiplies is not magic—it's the effect of compound interest. Imagine putting away $100 in your savings account at a local bank. If the bank pays a 5% annual interest rate, after one year, you will have $105. That extra $5 is the interest earned on your original deposit, known as the principal. Unlike simple interest, which only pays you based on your first $100 each year, compound interest pays you interest on both your principal and the interest you've already earned. In the second year, you earn interest not just on your $100, but also on the $5 from the first year. So now, your account grows by another $5.25, making your total $110.25 at the end of year two. Each year, the amount of interest gets larger, even if you don't add any more money.

Picture a chart with four columns—Year, Starting Balance, Interest Added, and New Balance. In year one, the starting balance is $100. The interest added is $5. By the end of the year, your new balance is $105. In year two, your starting balance is $105. The interest now is 5% of $105, which is $5.25, leaving you with $110.25. As each year passes, the interest column in this chart gets a little bigger, all by itself, even though the principal never changes. Over a handful of years, the effect is subtle. Over ten or twenty years, it's hard to believe how the growth speeds up.

With simple interest, you would only ever get 5% of $100 each year—$5. After five years, you'd have $125. But with compound interest, your money doesn't just move forward at a steady pace; it speeds up. After five years, you would have about $127.63, already ahead of simple interest. This difference keeps widening the longer you leave your money alone. A chart showing both simple and compound growth would start with the lines close together, but as time moves on, the line for compound interest bends upward faster and faster, while the simple interest line remains a gentle, steady climb.

Let's look at an everyday example on a slightly larger scale. If you start by investing $1,000 at an 8% interest rate, at the end of the first year you will have $1,080. In the second year, you add another $1,000. Your new total is $2,080, and you earn 8% of this amount, which is $166.40. Now, your balance is $2,246.40. In year three, you start with $2,246.40, add another $1,000, bringing the total to $3,246.40. Earning 8% interest again gives you $259.71, taking your total to $3,506.11. A visual step-by-step table would show the starting value growing larger each year, not only from your own contributions but also from the snowballing interest [3]. Soon, the yearly gain from interest outpaces the amount you are adding yourself.

The real magic of compound interest comes alive over long periods. Saving $1,000 every year and earning 8% a year means that, with patience, after ten years, the total interest earned is already larger than $8,000; after 20 years, the interest balloons to nearly $42,000; at 30 years, nearly $90,000; and at 40 years, compound interest alone grows to $205,000, dwarfing your $40,000 in contributions. On any chart tracking your balance over time, the amount from interest swells dramatically, overtaking the line representing your savings. What starts as a slow trickle becomes a powerful wave.

This effect explains why so many financial experts recommend starting to save as early as possible, even if the amounts feel small. It's not about putting away huge sums right away. It's about giving your money time to grow on itself. Consider two savers: one starts at age 20, regularly saving a modest $100 a month at a 4% annual interest rate, compounded monthly. By age 65, this steady saver has about $151,550, having put in just $54,100. Another person, starting at age 50, invests $5,000 upfront, plus $500 each month for 15 years. Even with nearly double the total contributions, this late starter ends up with only $132,147 at age 65 [4].

Charts and graphs from these real-life stories would show the early starter's money curving upward, pulling away from the late saver. Year after year, the compounding effect creates a gap that grows wider and wider, proving that time is far more valuable than making large deposits later to "catch up." This gentle but constant upward curve captures why compound interest is often called magical, even if the process is pure math.

Holding off on saving narrows the time window that allows compounding to do its work. The later you begin, the less chance your interest has to multiply and build momentum, making it much harder to reach those impressive financial goals.

What Waiting Really Costs: Opportunity Lost and Hands-On Compounding Exercise

Picture two friends, Maya and Chris. Maya starts saving for retirement as soon as she lands her first job at 22, putting away $100 every month into a retirement account that earns 7% yearly interest. Chris is busy with other expenses and waits until age 32 before starting his own savings journey, contributing the same $100 per month and earning the same 7% interest. Both keep up these savings habits until they turn 62. That's 40 years for Maya and just 30 for Chris.

At age 62, Maya's account has grown to about $240,000—she contributed $48,000 in total, but over three-quarters of her total came from the magic of compound interest. Chris saves for 30 years, contributing $36,000. Even after three decades, his account reaches only about $112,000. The ten-year delay cost Chris not just ten years of $100 contributions, but also cost him nearly $130,000 in lost growth—the money that would have been "earning money" for itself during that extra decade. Most people think of the cost of waiting as just what they didn't put in. In reality, the cost is all the compounding they missed while sitting on the sidelines [1].

Let's try flipping the roles. Assume both want to have at least $240,000 by age 62—the amount Maya ended up with. Chris, now starting at 32, realizes he must catch up. To reach the same goal, Chris must more than double his savings, putting away about $215 per month instead of $100, to give compound interest enough material to work on. Delaying means he must commit twice as much money just to catch up, which can be a tall order alongside new expenses like a mortgage or family needs. The extra years when interest is 'working' are like giving your money more seasons in the sun to grow and multiply, a true example of opportunity cost in action [2].

Now, let's think about a different scenario, one with a smaller monthly amount. Suppose Jenny, age 22, sets aside just $50 per month at 7%. At age 52, she'll have close to $60,000, even though she only contributed $18,000 over 30 years. But if she had started the same savings at age 32, her account would show only about $28,000 by age 52—a difference of more than $30,000, all coming from the extra decade of compounding. Even modest amounts make a dramatic difference when started early [1].

That ten-year gap is the whole lesson. A dollar saved at 25 has roughly twice as long to compound as a dollar saved at 35 – and no amount of saving more later fully closes that gap. The lesson is clear—the benefit of compound interest multiplies with time, far more than with higher monthly savings alone [2].

Here's a simple exercise to help you see your own savings story in action. The goal is to estimate how your monthly savings can grow with compound interest over time. All you need is a notebook, a calculator, or your phone.

1. Choose a monthly savings amount. Write down how much you could reasonably put aside each month, whether it's $25, $50, or $100. For our example, let's use $100 per month.
2. Decide on an annual interest rate. Many long-term investments, like stock market accounts, have averaged around 7% yearly returns, though this can vary. Write "7%" next to your savings amount.
3. Pick how many years you want to save. Write down your age now and the age when you hope to use the money—subtract to find the number of years. For this example, let's use 30 years.
4. Multiply your monthly amount by 12, then by the number of years. This gives your total contributions. $100 x 12 = $1,200 per year, $1,200 x 30 = $36,000 over 30 years.
5. Estimate the effect of compounding. Use a free online compounding calculator. These look like simple online forms where you enter your monthly contribution, interest rate, and number of years. They show two numbers: your total contributions and your total account value with interest. In our example, entering $100 monthly, 7% interest, and 30 years, you'll see a result of about $113,000.
6. Subtract your total contributions from the final amount. $113,000 – $36,000 = $77,000. This is the "extra" your money earned for you while you slept and lived your life, thanks to compound interest.

You can easily repeat these steps with your own numbers. If you prefer, search 'compound interest calculator' and look for tools that have clearly labeled boxes for 'monthly contribution,' 'interest rate,' and 'years invested.' Many of these even provide simple bar charts, which help people who learn best by seeing pictures.

Knowing how to make saving work for you is just the start. Soon, you'll learn fast mental shortcuts for guessing how quickly your money doubles, without a calculator or spreadsheet. For now, focus on the huge, quiet cost of waiting, and run the numbers yourself before moving on — seeing your own situation on paper is what makes this stick.

Simple Retirement Math: Tools, Analogies, and Your Own Milestones

Here's the fastest shortcut for estimating how long it takes money to double: the Rule of 72. Just divide the interest rate you see on your savings account or retirement plan into 72. The answer is the number of years for your savings to double. Say you've got a savings account promising 6% interest. Divide 72 by 6. That's 12 years—so if you keep your savings in that account and earn 6% interest every year, your money will double in 12 years. Try a slightly lower rate, like 4%. Divide 72 by 4. That's 18 years for your money to double. This trick is quick, easy, and saves you from grabbing a calculator or trying to memorize complex math formulas. It's like figuring out how many minutes it'll take for your pasta to cook by checking the box—72 is your "set it and forget it" number for money doubling.

Financial jargon can feel like trying to understand instructions in another language, so let's swap in some everyday imagery. Picture a jar of marbles. Your principal is the marbles already in the jar. Your "rate of return" is how many new marbles get added each year as a percentage of what's already there — add 6 marbles for every 100 already in the jar, and your return is 6%. The part people miss: next year, you're not just adding 6% of your original amount. You're adding 6% of the new, larger total — marbles earning marbles. Every marble or leaf added is like another mini-investment working for you all on its own.

Detailed steps for using the Rule of 72 and projecting long-term savings growth:

1. Find out your yearly interest rate (the rate of return on your investment or savings).
2. Divide 72 by your yearly interest rate. This answer is about how many years it will take for your money to double.
3. To see how consistent savings can grow, decide on the fixed amount you'll set aside each year, such as $500 or $1,000.
4. Use the Rule of 72 to estimate when your first deposit will double, then keep in mind each yearly deposit also begins its own journey of doubling and redoubling, the same way each year's marbles join the pile and start earning their own additions.
5. Write out or picture milestone years such as 10, 20, and 30 years from now, so you can estimate the future value of repeat savings.
6. For a hands-on illustration, walk through an example with friendly, round numbers.

Example story and calculation steps:

Meet Sam, a beginner saver who puts $500 every year into an account earning 6% compound interest. He wants to know how his money might grow over a few decades.

1. Sam checks his account's rate: 6%.
2. Sam uses the Rule of 72: 72 divided by 6 equals 12.
3. Sam realizes each $500 deposit will double after 12 years. His very first $500 from Year One grows to $1,000 in Year 13, then $2,000 in Year 25, and keeps going.
4. Every year, Sam adds another $500. Each deposit starts its own "doubling clock," but the earlier deposits double multiple times, while later ones have less time to grow before Sam retires.
5. The earlier deposits have had more time to compound, so they end up contributing disproportionately more to the final balance than the later ones — even though every deposit was the same $500.

Chart description for visualizing compounding growth

Here's what that looks like in real numbers. By Year 10, Sam has deposited $5,000 total, and his account is worth about $6,600. At

Year 20, total deposits reach $10,000, but compound interest has swelled the account to just over $19,900. By Year 30, Sam has deposited $15,000 in total, but his balance leaps to nearly $44,100. The key lesson from these numbers: It doesn't take flashy, one-time windfalls to grow wealth. Slow, steady savings—combined with time—yields much better results than stashing money sporadically. As explained in earlier scenario exercises, the longer you wait to start, the less time compounding has to work. That's why starting early beats waiting for the "perfect" moment, and why small, consistent steps always outweigh big, rare leaps in financial growth ([6]; [5]).

Budgeting a regular savings amount and sticking to it becomes a practical, powerful tool. You don't have to do complex math. With easy rules of thumb and a few simple calculations, anyone can chart a path to financial security without worrying that advanced skills or expert advice are required. The numbers do the heavy lifting, especially when you give them enough time to grow. The confidence you build through even basic exercises translates directly into peace of mind about the future—just as readers discovered in earlier hands-on steps ([5]; [6]).

Lessons Learned

Now that we understand the remarkable effect of compound interest and the importance of starting to save early, we can take confident steps toward building a secure financial future. Save something today, let it compound untouched, and the growth takes care of itself — quietly, and faster than it feels like it should. With simple tools like the Rule of 72 and clear examples to guide us, planning for retirement or other goals becomes less daunting and more achievable. This foundation not only helps us prepare wisely for what lies ahead but also opens the door to exploring more strategies that make managing and growing money a natural part of everyday life.

KEY TAKEAWAYS

- Compound interest is interest earned on your previous interest. It starts slowly and then accelerates — the longer you leave it alone, the faster it grows.
- The Rule of 72: divide 72 by your expected annual return to estimate how many years it takes for your money to double. At 7%, that's roughly ten years.

- Simple interest pays you a fixed amount based on your original deposit every year. Compound interest pays you more each year because your balance keeps growing. The difference becomes enormous over decades.
- Starting ten years earlier often outweighs contributing three times as much over fewer years. Time is your most powerful financial asset — more powerful than income level, investment skill, or market timing.
- Small, consistent deposits beat large, irregular ones. Automating your contributions removes the decision and keeps compounding working year-round, even when life gets busy.

Next up: The different types of retirement accounts available to you — and a plain-English guide to choosing the one that fits your situation.

Chapter 3: Types of Retirement Accounts: Which One's Your BFF?

Chapter at a Glance

What you´ ll learn in this chapter:

- The key difference between a Traditional 401(k) and a Roth 401(k) — and which type of earner each one tends to suit
- How Traditional IRAs and Roth IRAs work, including the 2025 income limits that determine who can contribute to each
- What a SEP-IRA and SIMPLE IRA are, and who they're designed for
- A simple decision framework to help you choose between account types without second-guessing yourself

Estimated reading time: 22 minutes

> **FIELD NOTE** *The "which account is best?" question has no universal answer — it depends on whether your tax rate is higher now or will be higher later. The good news is you don't have to guess. This chapter gives you a framework to work it out, and the option to use both types if you want to hedge your bets.*

When it comes to preparing for retirement, choosing the right savings accounts can feel like navigating a maze without a map. There are so many options—each with its own set of rules, benefits, and potential pitfalls—that it's easy to get overwhelmed or put off making decisions altogether. The real question isn't which account is "best" — it's which one matches your tax situation right now versus where you expect to land later. Get that wrong and you're not making a catastrophic mistake, just leaving some efficiency on the table. Get it right and it compounds for decades.

Traditional vs. Roth 401(k): Concepts, Features, and Choosing Situations

A Traditional 401(k) functions a bit like a workplace savings "superpower." When Jane, a 36-year-old marketing manager, signs up for her company's Traditional 401(k), she's setting aside a portion of every paycheck before taxes even touch it. If Jane decides to contribute $8,000 this year, that $8,000 doesn't count as part of her taxable income for the year. Let's say she earns $70,000; by contributing to her 401(k), she'll only owe income taxes on $62,000. This doesn't mean Jane gets out of paying tax altogether—instead, she's delaying it. The IRS is satisfied to wait until Jane withdraws her money in retirement, when the expectation is that she might be in a lower tax bracket. Today, during her higher-earning years, Jane lightens her current tax load, freeing up more money in her budget to cover other needs or maybe set aside for a family vacation [1].

But how does this really play out? Suppose Jane currently pays taxes in the 24% bracket, but expects that in retirement she'll live on less and fall into the 12% bracket. By stashing money in her Traditional 401(k), she avoids paying 24% tax now and, years later, pays just 12% when she takes money out. For Jane, that's a potentially big long-term win.

Employer matching is another appealing feature. Many companies will add to Jane's 401(k) contributions, sometimes matching dollar-for-dollar up to a limit, amplifying her savings. However, there's a small catch—eventually, usually starting at age 73, the IRS asks for its slice. Jane must start withdrawing, known as required minimum distributions (RMDs), and each dollar becomes taxable income at that point [6].

A Roth 401(k) flips some of these mechanics around. When Carlos, age 25 and just starting his tech career, signs up for his company's Roth 401(k), he agrees to pay taxes on his contributions up front. Money comes in from his paycheck after taxes are withheld. If Carlos contributes $6,000 this year from his $50,000 salary, he'll still owe taxes on the whole $50,000. But here's the twist—when Carlos retires decades later, every penny he withdraws from his Roth 401(k), including all the growth and investment gains, is completely tax-free.

This perk can be especially valuable if Carlos's income rises over time and he expects his tax rate in retirement to go up. By locking in today's lower tax rate, he builds a future "tax-free zone" for himself.

Think about Carlos's situation: at age 25, he's in a relatively low tax bracket. He expects to move up in his career and earn more, possibly jumping into higher brackets down the road. With the Roth 401(k), Carlos is betting on his own upward mobility. By paying taxes early, he sidesteps larger tax bills in the future, keeping more of his retirement savings for himself [1].

Both the Traditional and Roth 401(k) accounts allow you to invest in a range of options—mutual funds, stocks, bonds—though you're limited to what your employer's plan offers. And both accounts now allow higher contribution limits than IRAs, making them the go-to tools for building larger retirement savings [6].

Deciding Which Account is Your Best Fit

To pick the right 401(k) for your needs, start by asking:

- Is my current tax rate higher or lower than what I expect in retirement?
- Am I early in my career and expecting raises, or am I at my peak or nearing retirement?
- Would I like tax relief today, or would future tax-free withdrawals benefit me more?
- Do I plan to stay in the same city, state, or country—where tax rules may change?

Say you're in your 40s, earning $90,000 a year, and planning to work another two decades. If you're in a higher bracket now and think you'll downsize later, a Traditional 401(k) gives current-year relief and leverages a possible lower future tax bracket. On the other hand, if you're 28, fresh out of grad school, and see plenty of promotions ahead, a Roth 401(k) likely maximizes your tax-free withdrawal potential when you're making much more.

Here's a side-by-side example. Alex, 45, is a senior nurse making $100,000 and expects a modest lifestyle in retirement. She might favor a Traditional 401(k). Meanwhile, Jamie, 27, is an engineer with entry-level pay who anticipates steady raises. "For Jamie, a Roth 401(k) may be attractive—pay tax now at a lower rate, then potentially enjoy qualified Roth withdrawals tax-free later. Employer matching contributions, however, are not automatically tax-free just because the employee chooses Roth treatment; their tax treatment depends on the plan's rules.

As readers continue, they'll discover practical tools and story-driven scenarios to make these choices feel even more approachable. Step-by-step visuals and easy examples will help avoid common slip-ups and show how the right decision now steers retirement dreams in the right direction ([6]; [1]).

Practical Tools & Humorous Scenarios for Choosing Between 401(k) Options

Some people say choosing between a Traditional and Roth 401(k) is a bit like picking a superhero for your team. Picture Sam—a new grad starting her first job—meeting her HR rep, who explains that "team Traditional" gives you super savings on taxes now, while "team Roth" promises those tax savings after you leave the workforce. Both have perks, but which powers fit Sam's current life best?

Traditional 401(k)s let you save before taxes come out, so your paycheck stretches a little more. It's as if you get a coupon for your taxes now, promising to settle the bill when you're older and maybe in a lower tax bracket. Roth 401(k)s are the opposite: you pay Uncle Sam from the start, and once your money grows and you finally need it in retirement, it's all yours—no taxes due. These basics seem simple, but real life complicates them quickly.

Take Jake, who's enjoying peak years of earning as a mid-career engineer. He wonders, "Should I take my tax break now or later?" Jake's HR emails a decision table, which he prints out and sticks to his fridge:

Life Stage & Income	Traditional 401(k)	Roth 401(k)
-----------------------------	---------------------------------	-------------------------------
Young, low income	Not usually ideal	Strong candidate
Early/mid-career, stable	Good for high current earners	Consider as income grows

Approaching retirement, high	Maximizes current tax benefit	Prefers future tax-free gains

Jake reads: If you're just starting out or your income is on the lower side, Roth 401(k)s are often the go-to because you're paying tax on dollars that would be taxed little anyway. It's like buying fairground tickets when prices are cheap and using them much later when the price goes up. But as your career progresses, and your income (and tax rate) climbs, Traditional 401(k)s can offer a bigger upfront savings. Many financial planners agree with this approach, since high earners save the most by deferring taxes [2].

Let's jump to Maya, nearing retirement. She's saved diligently using her Traditional 401(k). Now, as she prepares to withdraw money, she finds her tax bill is smaller than the rate she paid decades ago. She smiles, remembering the advice: it's often best to defer taxes when you're earning more and pay them later when you possibly drop into a lower bracket [3]. Maya also considers tax diversity. If she adds Roth savings through backdoor Roth IRA contributions, she gets flexibility, choosing from both taxable and tax-free sources in retirement [2].

But what if you make the wrong call? Barry, a bustling young consultant, thinks "taxes are confusing—I'll just pick both." He doesn't coordinate his contributions, ends up exceeding IRS limits by mistake, and must pay a penalty. Or he saves a bunch in a Traditional 401(k), then does a Roth conversion in a high-income year, doubling up on taxes. Barry's oops moment is a classic reminder: matching the right account to the right income profile and double-checking contribution limits can save a headache [2].

Having a mix of Roth and Traditional accounts can also be like owning both rain boots and sunglasses. You'll be prepared for whatever tax "weather" hits in retirement. No one knows if future tax laws will change, but having both options can help you reduce your tax bill year-to-year [3]. If you're a part-timer planning to retire early, you might convert Traditional to Roth during lower earning years to "fill up" those lower tax brackets, which is like buying items on sale rather than at full price later on [2].

Look at Ella, a military doctor and seasoned planner. During residency, she maxed out her Roth 401(k) because her tax rate was low. Years later, as an attending physician, she shifted to Traditional 401(k) contributions. This method let her take the "best of both worlds," earning her the nickname "Tax Rate Ninja" among friends [2]. For couples or anyone with variable income, striking this balance is key.

If you ever feel stumped, remember you don't have to decide alone. Reach out to a financial planner or use tools offered by your workplace to chart your current and future tax rates. Be honest about your savings habits—people who save more than 20% of their income may lean a little more to Roth, while those saving less often benefit from tax-deferred accounts [2].

As readers like Maya wrap up their 401(k) decision, they often wonder, "What if I want more flexibility, or what if I start freelancing?" That curiosity is what leads many to investigate other savings options, such as IRAs, especially for those who aren't tied to a single employer or want to diversify even further. Each strategy builds on the confidence you've gained, opening up new ways to strengthen your retirement safety net and shape your future with the calm certainty of a seasoned saver.

IRAs: Options Breakdown, Features, and Comparison Table

Storytelling remains a key tool for making financial decisions feel less daunting. Just as comparing 401(k) options helped many people, breaking down the main types of IRAs can guide someone toward the right choice for their future. Retirement planning isn't just for experts, and understanding IRAs doesn't require a math degree. Instead, practical comparisons, relatable scenarios, and concrete differences can make the process clear and engaging.

The Traditional IRA is often the first account people hear about. Its main appeal lies in the possibility of deducting contributions from current taxable income. Someone midway through their career, earning enough to sit solidly in a mid-range tax bracket, is a good candidate: putting money into a Traditional IRA lowers this year's tax bill.These contributions grow without being taxed until retirement. At that point, the IRS takes taxes on each withdrawal as ordinary income. This feature makes the Traditional IRA attractive to individuals expecting to be in a lower tax bracket when retired than during their highest earning years. For someone who needs a current tax break but doesn't mind paying taxes on withdrawals later, this account can be a clear win [5].

The Roth IRA offers a different kind of benefit. Instead of reducing taxable income today, money contributed to a Roth IRA comes from dollars already taxed. Because no up-front deduction exists, the value of a Roth IRA shows up later. Qualified withdrawals—usually those made after age 59½ and when the account has been held at least five years—are completely tax-free. This feature gives Roth IRAs power for people who expect their tax rate to rise over time or who enjoy the idea of tax-free income in retirement. Younger earners, or those early in their careers, often appreciate the chance to let their investments grow for decades without the looming worry of future taxation. Another unique Roth advantage is no requirement to take minimum withdrawals during the owner's lifetime, providing flexibility and more control over when and how to use these savings [4].

Then there are SEP IRAs and SIMPLE IRAs. Both are designed with self-employed individuals, freelancers, and small business owners in mind. These workers may not have access to typical employer-sponsored accounts, so these IRA types open new doors to substantial retirement savings.

A SEP IRA—short for Simplified Employee Pension—allows higher contribution limits than either Traditional or Roth IRAs. It's built for the self-employed and small business owners: contribute up to 25% of net earnings, up to an IRS-set limit. Contributions are usually tax-deductible, and like the Traditional IRA, taxes on growth get deferred until money comes out in retirement. Employers alone make contributions to employee SEPs, so employees don't contribute directly, but those with self-employment income can play both roles [5].

SIMPLE IRAs, or Savings Incentive Match Plans for Employees, streamline the retirement process for businesses with 100 or fewer workers. These plans let both the employer and the employees put away money, with the added bonus of required employer contributions. An employer can match up to 3% of an employee's compensation or make a 2% nonelective contribution for every eligible worker, which means employees get retirement contributions even if they don't put in any of their own money. This simplifies saving and can encourage participation, especially among small companies lacking the resources for more complex retirement plans. For example, if someone has a side business employing a handful of staff, a SIMPLE IRA could offer affordable and predictable retirement benefits, boosting morale and helping them save at the same time [5].

Here's a quick comparison of key IRA features to help match life situations with the right account:

- Traditional IRA: Tax-deductible contributions; required minimum distributions generally begin at age 73, or age 75 for individuals born in 1960 or later, depending on current IRS rules; taxed withdrawals; suited for those seeking immediate tax savings.
- Roth IRA: After-tax contributions; no required minimum withdrawals for original owners; tax-free qualified withdrawals; ideal for younger savers or people expecting higher taxes later.
- SEP IRA: Employer-funded; very high contribution limits; pre-tax savings; great for small business owners and freelancers wanting to maximize yearly savings.
- SIMPLE IRA: For small businesses under 100 employees; both employer and employee can contribute; required employer match or 2% contribution; straightforward, with less paperwork and no annual filing for the employer.

Eligibility, contribution limits, and withdrawal rules shape which IRA makes sense for each person. Whether a full-time worker craving a tax break, a young professional preparing for decades of growth, or a small business owner mixing retirement and payroll solutions, there's a good match out there. By considering career stage, earnings, and future tax expectations, the process of picking an IRA can feel just as comfortable and logical as choosing the right 401(k), putting retirement goals within easy reach ([4]; [5]).

KEY TAKEAWAYS

- Traditional accounts (401(k) and Traditional IRA) give you a tax break today but require you to pay income tax on withdrawals in retirement. Roth accounts use money you've already paid tax on, so qualified withdrawals later are completely tax-free.
- The best choice usually comes down to one question: do you expect your tax rate to be higher now, or higher in retirement? If higher now, lean Traditional. If higher later, lean Roth. If you're not sure, a mix of both gives you flexibility.
- For 2025, Roth IRA contributions begin to phase out at a modified adjusted gross income of $150,000 for single filers and $236,000 for married filing jointly. If you're above these thresholds, a

backdoor Roth conversion may still be an option – discussed in Chapter 9.

- Self-employed or running a small business? A SEP-IRA lets you contribute up to 25% of your net self-employment income, with a 2025 ceiling of $70,000. That's significantly more than a standard IRA allows.
- You don't have to pick just one. Many people hold a workplace 401(k) and a personal IRA simultaneously, using each for different tax advantages.

Next up: How to actually open these accounts and make your first contribution – without the paperwork confusion.

Chapter 4: Starting Strong: Opening and Funding Your Accounts

Chapter at a Glance

What you´ ll learn in this chapter:

- How to navigate your employer's 401(k) enrollment forms — what each section is actually asking, and why it matters
- How to open an IRA on your own and which type of provider (bank, broker, or robo-advisor) might suit you best
- Why naming a beneficiary is one of the most important things you'll do — and what happens if you skip it
- The default investment trap: what your employer may automatically put your money into, and how to take control

Estimated reading time: 20 minutes

FIELD NOTE *Most people fill out their 401(k) enrollment form in ten minutes during onboarding, tick the boxes, and never look at it again. A few small decisions made on that form — particularly your contribution percentage and your investment selection — can be worth tens of thousands of dollars over time. This chapter makes sure you know what you're signing.*

Most people sign their 401(k) enrollment form the same way they click "accept" on a software update — fast, without reading it, eager to get back to their actual job. That's how a default contribution rate of 3% becomes a permanent decision nobody actually made. This chapter is about making those choices on purpose instead of by accident.

Navigating 401(k) Enrollment and Contribution Choices

Walking into a new job with a stack of forms in your hand, you might see an invitation to enroll in your company's 401(k) plan tucked into your onboarding paperwork or emailed through your employer's HR portal. For many people, the first look at this unfamiliar document brings up lots of questions. If you feel this way, you're not alone—a 401(k) can seem confusing at the start, but the process of signing up is usually pretty simple once you know what to expect.

New employees often receive a welcome packet or an email with information about benefits. In almost every company, there is a section explaining how to sign up for the workplace retirement plan. Sometimes there's a direct link to an online enrollment site. Other times, a paper form is included for you to fill out and return to Human Resources. No matter the format, the beginning steps are similar across companies.

When you open up the enrollment form, you'll start by entering the basics: your full name, birthdate, and Social Security number. This information is needed to set up your account and make sure it's tied to your tax records. Many forms will ask for your home address and a personal email. These details are how the retirement plan provider contacts you and sends account information.

The next section asks what percentage of your paycheck you want to contribute to the 401(k). This is where many people pause—what does it mean to contribute 3%, 6%, or 10%? Think of your paycheck as a pizza. Deciding what percentage to save is like choosing how many slices to set aside for later. If your paycheck is $2,000 and you choose 5%, then $100 will be placed in your 401(k) each pay period, before taxes are taken out [6]. Most forms include a simple menu or box: you just enter a number, and often you can change this number later.

A common part of the process involves naming a beneficiary. This person would inherit your 401(k) balance if something should happen to you. Usually, people name a spouse, family member, or close friend. There may be a space to list a backup, called a contingent beneficiary. While it can feel odd to think about, this step is important for protecting your money.

Next, you'll adjust your investment choices. The form might present a set of pre-selected options, such as how aggressively you want your money invested (for example, a target date fund based on your age, or a mix of stocks and bonds). If you don't make a choice, the plan might automatically put your funds into a default investment meant to suit your expected retirement year [1]. You can usually return later to personalize your investments, but it helps to review the available options, and ask HR or your plan provider if there's anything you don't understand.

To make the process smoother, gather needed information before sitting down—this might include your Social Security card and the contact information of anyone you want to list as a beneficiary. Review all materials your employer sends, since they often contain explanations or comparisons of contribution levels, investment choices, and frequently asked questions. If you feel stuck, reach out to HR or an employee helpline early on. They're used to helping first-timers, and your question is probably one they've heard many times before.

Avoid common pitfalls by double-checking the form for skipped fields, which can cause delays, or unclear handwriting if it's paper. You usually won't need your bank account details for a 401(k), since contributions are pulled straight from your paycheck, making this easier than setting up direct deposit at a bank. Think of completing the enrollment like following a simple "recipe"—with basic ingredients like your name, Social Security number, and contribution choice coming together to help you get started.

Deciding how much to contribute often brings up the worry of not saving enough or taking home too little pay. The best approach for beginners is to start with a percentage that feels comfortable. Even 1% or 2% is worth doing now — you can raise it later, but you can't get back the years you didn't start. For example, if you pick 3% and earn $40,000 per year, about $1,200 would be set aside each year for your retirement—before taxes. Over years, this sum, plus investment growth, can build into something much greater than its starting size [1].

There's no one-size-fits-all answer, and you can usually change your contribution rate later. Many people set a yearly reminder to review and increase their savings with each raise or during annual benefits enrollment. Starting small and building up means you begin building a good saving habit now, without feeling stressed or overwhelmed. Each step gets you closer to the comfort and security that a well-funded retirement can offer ([6]; [1]).

Maximizing Employer Matching and Beginning Your IRA Journey

When it comes to saving for retirement, few things are as satisfying as letting your money work quietly behind the scenes—and employer matching is a prime example of this. Employer matching simply means your boss will add extra money to your 401(k) account based on how much you put in yourself. Think of it as walking into a local bakery, buying one donut, and the baker saying, "Since you bought one, I'll give you a second one for free." If given the chance, you wouldn't leave that free donut behind. In retirement saving, employer matching is the "free donut" many workers leave untouched just by not signing up or by not contributing enough. For beginners, a common match is that the employer puts in fifty cents for every dollar you contribute, up to 6% of your salary. Others match dollar-for-dollar up to a certain amount. Imagine you earn $40,000 a year. If your company offers a match of 100% for the first 6% you contribute, that's $2,400 a year you can get just by putting in $2,400 yourself. Your total grows to $4,800, instantly.

If you only chip in 3%, or $1,200, your company only matches that amount, so your "free money" is cut in half. Your goal should always be to contribute at least enough to get the highest match offered. One way to do this is to look at your paycheck and see how much 6% is. If you set it up, the money comes out before you can spend it elsewhere. For anyone just starting out, it helps to think of this automatic contribution like a streaming service subscription—you barely notice it, but it adds up over time, and in this case, it grows with the bonus from your employer ([2]; [3]).

Picture a simple scene called "First Paycheck Reimagined." On one side, there's your paycheck before you sign up for the 401(k). Imagine you bring home $1,200 every two weeks. All your take-home pay is ready for bills, groceries, or a new pair of shoes. Now, after you start contributing 6% of your salary ($72 per paycheck), your take-home drops—to $1,128. The difference each payday is about what you'd spend on a dinner out. But while you're bringing home a little less, your retirement savings are working harder. With each paycheck, $72 goes into your account, and your employer puts another $72 right beside it. The "missing dinner" from your take-home pay becomes a pair of contributions that will grow over the years, thanks to investment returns.

If your budget feels tight, even starting with a 3% contribution helps lay a foundation. Over time you can nudge your contribution higher, chasing that full match at your own pace. Every percentage point you add gets matched at the same pace by your employer, for as long as you're both contributing. Once you get used to seeing that smaller paycheck, it quickly becomes your new normal, and your savings snowball quietly in the background ([2]; [3]).

When opening an IRA, the choice of provider can seem like walking into a room full of quirky hosts. At one side is the bank, standing tall in a stiff suit. Banks are the old-school friend—predictable, trustworthy, but sometimes not as lively when it comes to growing your savings. You know your money is in a safe, familiar place. Banks often offer IRAs with limited investments, such as CDs, and sometimes charge higher fees. Next to the bank, brokers stroll through in casual blazers, pockets full of investment tools. Brokers are like that enthusiastic neighbor who wants to help you with home projects—knowledgeable and happy to guide you, but you have to pick up the hammer yourself. With a broker, there's access to more investment choices, from stocks to bonds and mutual funds. Fees can be low, especially with online brokers, but there's more responsibility on your shoulders to choose and manage investments.

Then there's the robo-advisor, breezing in on a scooter, phone in hand, algorithms buzzing beneath a slick appearance. Robo-advisors are modern and hands-off—they automate everything and do the heavy lifting for you, adjusting your investments as needed for a small, clear fee. Perfect for anyone who wants their retirement savings to "just happen" in the background, with very little fuss. Your comfort level matters most here. Do you like having an expert to call, or do you want everything handled by a friendly robot while you sip your morning coffee? Do you prefer a face behind a desk or a sleek app on your phone? Consider the fees—some charge a fixed amount each year, while others take a small slice of your investments. Look at how quickly you can get help if you're stuck or confused.

Once you've picked your provider—whether it's the sturdy bank, hands-on broker, or breezy robo-advisor—the steps to open an IRA are straightforward. You'll gather a few personal details, decide how much to start with, and select how you want your savings invested. Each decision moves you closer to taking full advantage of your chosen account, making your future more secure and your next financial steps easier to take ([2]; [3]).

Step-by-Step IRA Setup and Contribution Guide

Gaining a sense of momentum feels satisfying, especially after learning the basics of retirement accounts and seeing how even small steps can yield long-term rewards. The hardest part is getting started. Once your account is open and your first contribution is in, the next steps — adjusting your percentage, picking investments — get easier, and most banks and apps walk you through each one. At this point, you are ready to navigate the process of opening your first IRA with confidence.

Preparation makes the process easier and faster. Before you begin, gather the following documents and information:

- Social Security Number: Needed for identity verification and tax reporting.
- Government-issued photo ID: For confirming your identity (useful if there's a security step that asks you to upload a photo).
- Employer and income details: Required in some cases to check eligibility, especially for Roth IRAs.
- Bank account info: To transfer funds and set up contributions.

Having everything in one spot, maybe inside a manila folder or scanned onto your laptop, helps smooth out the application process. Expect providers to use your Social Security Number to report contributions to the IRS and use your ID to match your identity for security. Bank information creates an electronic link for easy transfers. Providers usually walk you through each section online, indicating what is required with helpful progress bars and checklists so you can watch your progress in real time [4].

Choosing between a Traditional and Roth IRA comes next. A Traditional IRA allows you to deduct contributions from your taxes in the year you make them, which means you lower your current taxable income but pay taxes when you retire and start withdrawing funds. Roth IRAs work differently – money is contributed after taxes, so withdrawals in retirement (including the growth) are tax-free, provided certain conditions are met. Consider a young worker at the start of their career with a lower current income; they might favor a Roth IRA since their taxes are lower now and tax-free withdrawals in the future are attractive. By contrast, someone making more mid-career or expecting a lower tax bracket after retirement might prefer a Traditional IRA for the upfront deduction. These choices come down to your income, how much you expect your income to grow, and what feels best for your future plans [5].

The step-by-step process to actually open the account is designed to be user-friendly. Most platforms and brokerages offer online forms so you can apply from the comfort of home. Typically, you start by creating an account with a username and password, following the on-screen prompts to fill in your personal info, and verifying your identity, sometimes by uploading a picture of your driver's license or answering questions about your recent addresses. You'll enter your employment details and select whether you want a Traditional or Roth IRA. You'll link your checking or savings account for deposits by providing your routing and account numbers. If your provider's website shows a checklist, you'll see boxes getting checked off as each stage is completed, giving a sense of progress.

Once your IRA is created, making the first contribution is the next milestone. Many online platforms prompt you right away: "Make your first contribution now." You can usually type in a one-time dollar amount—start with $100 or $250—and select your linked bank account. Some providers let you set up a secure bank transfer with a few taps. Even $50 gets you started and counts toward your goals. You will receive a confirmation, usually by email or a dashboard notification, so you know everything went through smoothly ([4]; [5]).

Setting up recurring contributions is a smart tactic. Think about it like a gym membership or auto-pay for monthly bills—choose a schedule, like the first Friday of every month or with every paycheck. Consistency matters more than size; $30, $50, or $100 per month adds up, especially with the power of compounding over the years. Align the timing with your payday or budgeting cycle to keep cash flow simple. Many people find this habit makes saving feel automatic and worry-free, helping to build a strong retirement fund.

Understanding fees and minimum requirements will help you avoid costly surprises. IRAs may have minimum opening balances, which vary by provider. Provider A may require $500 to get started, Provider B might have no minimum, and Provider C could require $1,000. Think of three columns on a checklist: provider name, minimum opening amount, ongoing minimum. Some providers will also charge "maintenance" or "administration" fees, often between $10 and $50 per year. Transaction fees may be charged each time you buy or sell an investment. Low or no-fee options exist, so comparing these side by side can help you make a wise choice. For instance, if Provider B has no minimum but charges $25 yearly, while Provider A needs $500 but charges nothing, it's easy to weigh what works best for you. If you save $50 a month, but pay $25 yearly, by the end of the year you've paid 4% in fees—lower fees leave more money compounding for your future [4].

Every small decision and step builds confidence. By keeping all paperwork within reach and watching your progress, the path to a fully funded IRA feels achievable. Each contribution, no matter how small, is a move forward into a more secure financial future [5].

KEY TAKEAWAYS

- Enrolling in a 401(k) is usually simpler than it looks. The form asks for your basic details, your contribution percentage, a beneficiary, and your investment preferences. Each of these deserves a few minutes of thought rather than a quick default selection.
- Always name a beneficiary. Without one, your account may be tied up in probate, and the money may not reach the people you intend it to. Review this designation whenever your circumstances change.
- When opening an IRA, your three main provider options are banks (safe but limited investment choices), brokers (wider choices, more responsibility on you), and robo-advisors (automated, low-maintenance, small fee). Choose based on how hands-on you want to be.
- Don't let your employer's auto-enrollment settings run unchecked. Defaulting to a 3% contribution when a 6% contribution would capture the full match leaves money on the table from day one.

- Recurring, automated contributions are the most reliable savings habit. Treat it like a bill that gets paid first, every payday.

Next up: How to get the most out of every dollar you contribute — including a complete breakdown of how matching programs actually work.

Chapter 5: Contributions and Matching: Maximizing Every Dollar

Chapter at a Glance

What you′ ll learn in this chapter:

- The 2025 401(k) employee contribution limit, and the catch-up amount available to anyone aged 50 or older
- Exactly how employer matching programs work — with a breakdown of the most common formulas companies use
- The mistakes people most commonly make with contributions — and how to avoid each one
- IRA contribution limits, income-based deductibility rules, and the best timing strategy for your deposits

Estimated reading time: 22 minutes

> **FIELD NOTE** *The employer match is the one area of personal finance where the advice is almost always the same regardless of your situation: get all of it. Whatever minimum contribution is required to trigger your employer's full match — that's your floor, not your ceiling. Everything above that is a bonus.*

Many people know that saving for retirement is important, yet many also struggle to understand how to make their money work harder once it's in a savings account. It can feel confusing to figure out how employer benefits like 401(k) matching work or how to decide the best way to contribute to an IRA without missing out on valuable opportunities. Without clear guidance, it's easy to leave money on the table or worry about accidentally making costly mistakes.

The employer match is the one piece of this chapter where there's no real debate. Everything else is optimization; that part is just leaving money on the table if you skip it.

401(k) Matching Fundamentals and Maximizing Value

Most workplaces that offer a 401(k) retirement plan also want to sweeten the deal with something known as employer matching. At its core, this is a promise: for every dollar you stash away in your 401(k), the company will also chip in, matching your savings up to a certain amount. Imagine walking into a grocery store, buying an apple, and then watching the grocer toss in a second, free of charge. Employer matching works in a very similar, delightfully simple way.

Suppose you earn $50,000 a year. Your employer announces they'll match 50% of what you contribute to your 401(k), but only up to 6% of your salary. Let's break that down. Six percent of your salary is $3,000. If you put in $3,000 over the course of the year—a doable $250 each month—your employer will tack on another $1,500. It's their way of rewarding you for thinking ahead. Now, if you contribute more than $3,000, say $4,000, your employer's match still tops out at $1,500, because their contribution only matches up to the first 6% of your salary. It's free money that's capped, but free money all the same ([1]; [2]).

Picture yourself working in an office with a vending machine that, once every paycheck, offers you a bonus snack if you buy your favorite bag of chips. Refusing those extra snacks just doesn't make sense. Employer matching is the retirement equivalent of not leaving snacks behind. For every dollar you set aside, your company is working alongside you, turning your personal effort into a tag-team victory. Together, your contributions and theirs build your nest egg faster.

Employers offer different types of matches, but most fall into two main styles: dollar-for-dollar or percentage-based. A dollar-for-dollar match means if you put in $2,000, your company adds $2,000 to your 401(k)—as long as it's within their set maximum. For percentage-based matches, your employer might promise to match half of what you contribute, as in the earlier example, or perhaps 100% of the first 4% of pay, and then 50% for the next 2%. It's a bit like a buy-one-get-one, but sometimes with a slight twist—one slice of pizza per person, unless you eat faster, then they offer half-slices after that.

Let's look at some practical math. Suppose you make $60,000 a year. Your company offers a dollar-for-dollar match up to 5% of your salary. Five percent of $60,000 is $3,000. If you contribute $3,000 over the year, you get a full $3,000 extra, making your total annual savings $6,000, not even counting investment growth ([1]; [2]). If you decide that $3,000 is too much and only contribute $2,000, your employer matches just $2,000. You've essentially left $1,000 untouched—like turning down three months of free coffee at work.

Why does this matter so much? Because every dollar you and your employer set aside is invested, often in funds that grow over time. The magic word here is compounding. As your account earns interest or returns, those returns also start earning returns. Your contribution earns a return, the employer's match earns its own return, and those returns earn returns of their own. Over decades, that's the difference between doubling your money and quadrupling it.

Now imagine someone who steadily contributes enough every year to get their employer's full match. If the total contribution each year is $6,000 and the average annual return on those investments is 7%, after ten years that original $6,000 blossoms to about $83,000. After twenty years, it's grown to roughly $246,000. In thirty years, they are sitting on more than $580,000—purely from making sure they never miss a matching dollar and letting time do the rest ([1]; [2]).

Skipping out on your company's matching program can be a costly mistake. It's the financial version of saying no thanks to a free pizza party and then buying your own lunch instead. Yet, research shows that about half of workers don't contribute enough to get the full match, and some don't sign up for the 401(k) at all, despite how generous employer matching can be [1]. Some folks may not realize this matching money gets them ahead twice—once when the employer adds funds, and again as that cash earns investment gains over decades. Understanding how employer matching works is the first step toward making the most of every dollar you save for your future.

Avoiding Common Pitfalls and Optimizing Your 401(k)

Many workers understand that employer matching is one of the primary benefits of a 401(k) plan, yet subtle oversights and timing mistakes can seriously limit the value received from this feature. Missing out on part—or all—of the employer's matching contribution is a surprisingly common but costly mistake. For example, suppose an employer matches 100% of an employee's 401(k) contribution up to 5% of their salary. If an employee earning $80,000 a year decides to contribute only 3% of their income, they put away $2,400 for the year. However, the employer would only match that $2,400, leaving an additional $1,600 in unmatched employer contributions on the table. That difference, compounded over a 25–30 year career, could amount to hundreds of thousands of dollars in lost retirement growth, showing just how vital it is to hit the full match threshold each year [6].

Failing to enroll promptly in a 401(k) or postponing contributions is another often-overlooked pitfall. Consider a newly hired employee who waits several months before enrolling in their company's plan. During this period, not only are they missing out on personal contributions, but they forfeit the employer's matching funds for each missed pay period. Even short lapses can add up quickly, especially when factoring in the compounding effect—the snowballing of investment returns over time—which depends heavily on both how much and how early someone contributes.

Some workers also set their contribution rates just under the threshold required for full matching, perhaps misinformed about the exact terms of their employer's policy or simply underestimating the impact of a small difference. For example, if the match maxes out at 6% of pay, but an employee contributes 5%, they leave a full percentage point of employer money unclaimed. That kind of oversight, while seemingly minor, repeats itself each year and steadily saps the strength of long-term savings growth [3].

A simple comparison tool makes the benefits of optimizing contributions easier to grasp. Think of three employees with identical salaries of $75,000 per year and a plan that offers a dollar-for-dollar match up to 5%. The first employee contributes 3% ($2,250), the second 5% ($3,750), and the third 6% ($4,500). Their employers then match only up to the 5% level:

- Employee A: Contributes $2,250, employer matches $2,250, $4,500 total annual savings
- Employee B: Contributes $3,750, employer matches $3,750, $7,500 total annual savings
- Employee C: Contributes $4,500, employer matches $3,750, $8,250 total annual savings

While Employee C personally contributes more, their additional $750 is unmatched, making Employee B's approach the optimal point for maximizing employer dollars. Over a three-decade career, even with modest investment growth, maximizing the full match threshold results in tens (or even hundreds) of thousands more at retirement compared to lower contribution levels ([3]; [6]).

To avoid these missteps, employees should first examine their plan documents, which detail matching formulas, eligibility criteria, and vesting schedules. Asking questions of the company's benefits coordinator can provide clarity on ambiguous points, such as waiting periods or phased matches. Many plans now allow for automatic enrollment or the setting up of recurring payroll deductions. Using these features reduces the risk of missed contributions due to oversight or forgetfulness.

Imagine two employees: Ava bookmarks her benefits portal and sets her 401(k) contributions to automatically deduct 6% of her pay starting with her first paycheck. Over the next five years, Ava captures the full match every year, seeing her account grow steadily. Her colleague, Ben, forgets to enroll for ten months and, when he does, sets his contribution slightly too low to receive the maximum match. Years later, Ben is dismayed to find that his retirement balance lags far behind Ava's, illustrating that small early decisions can have outsized long-term consequences.

Being aware of required minimum distribution (RMD) ages and new emergency withdrawal provisions can also help guide smart contribution decisions as retirement nears [6]. Employees who think ahead, reviewing plan rules annually and increasing their contribution rate with each raise, often finish their careers well ahead of those who procrastinate or underestimate the power of steady, matched savings.

Even the frequency of contributions—such as making smaller, regular deposits with each paycheck versus waiting until the year's end—can boost the compounding effect, especially if investment returns are reinvested immediately. In the next section, the focus shifts to how timing and incremental strategy choices in other retirement accounts, like IRAs, can further elevate savings outcomes for careful planners.

Mastering IRA Contribution Strategies for Smart Savings

Every year, the IRS sets limits on how much you can contribute to an Individual Retirement Account (IRA). For 2025, the maximum is $6,000 for anyone under 50. If you are 50 or older, you can add a "catch-up" contribution of $1,000, bringing your total limit to $7,000 [4]. Sometimes, these numbers increase slightly because of inflation adjustments. Anyone saving for retirement should always check the most recent limit for their age before adding money. Going over the IRS cap—even by a few dollars—can result in a 6% penalty on the excess contribution until you remove it. If you accidentally deposit too much, you need to withdraw the extra money, plus any earnings it made, before filing your tax return for that year. Knowing the limits can help you avoid surprise penalties, extra paperwork, and potential tax issues down the line [4].

When it comes to putting money into your IRA, there are two main ways to contribute: monthly or in a lump sum. Monthly funding—sometimes called dollar-cost averaging—means you divide your annual limit by twelve and deposit a smaller sum each month. Lump-sum investing is when you deposit the entire yearly amount at once, such as after receiving a bonus. For example, imagine you have $6,000 to invest this year. If the market goes up steadily, putting it in all at once might let your money grow more, because it's working for you sooner. However, if markets drop right after your lump-sum investment, your account value could fall before recovering. On the other hand, monthly investing spreads your risk across up and down months, which can feel safer if you're nervous about short-term drops.

Comparing Growth: Monthly vs. Lump-Sum

Scenario	Investment Method	Start Value	Growth Scenario (7%)	End Value
Steady market rise	Lump-sum	$6,000	7% annual	$6,420
Steady market rise	Monthly	$500/ month	7% annual	$6,235
Early-year market dip	Lump-sum	$6,000	Drops 10%, then recovers	$5,920
Early-year market dip	Monthly	$500/ month	Drops 10%, then recovers	$6,050

Monthly contributions may lead to a slightly lower return in a rising market, but they give you peace of mind by balancing gains and losses over time. Some savers prefer monthly installments because it aligns with their paychecks or helps them manage their budget. For example, if you get paid every two weeks, you could set up an automatic transfer of $250 every payday. Others might choose to invest in a lump sum after getting a tax return or work bonus. Either way, it's important to pick a method that matches your cash flow and comfort with risk [5].

Deductibility rules for traditional IRA contributions depend on income, filing status, and whether you or your spouse are covered by a workplace retirement plan. For example, a single person earning less than $83,000 in 2025 can deduct the full amount. If their income is between $83,000 and $103,000, only part of the contribution is deductible; above $103,000, none is deductible [4]. Now consider a married couple: if both spouses have workplace retirement plans, full deductibility usually ends at $136,000 of combined income and phases out above $156,000. If only one spouse is covered by a plan, these limits may be higher. This matters at tax time because deductible IRA contributions lower your taxable income, potentially decreasing what you owe and freeing up more money in your budget.

When income rises above these cutoffs, savers can still contribute to a traditional IRA but might lose most or all of the immediate tax break. For example, imagine Mark and Brianna, who are married and file jointly with a combined income of $140,000. Since this is above the $136,000 deductibility threshold for their situation, only a portion of their IRA contribution is deductible. If their income rises to $160,000, none of their IRA contributions are tax-deductible. This shift could mean they keep less cash in hand at tax time, so planning ahead is essential [4].

Step-by-Step IRA Contribution Exercise

1. **List all yearly income** (wages, side jobs, bonuses) on a blank sheet or spreadsheet.
2. **Write down basic monthly expenses**: rent or mortgage, utilities, groceries, transportation, debt payments, health insurance, and extras.
3. **Subtract expenses from income** to see how much is left for savings after covering needs.
4. **Check your age** to see if you qualify for the $1,000 catch-up contribution.
5. **Look up the IRS IRA deductibility chart** for your current year and see where your adjusted gross income fits. If you use online summaries, circle the row that matches your situation.
6. **Decide if your IRA contributions will be fully deductible, partially deductible, or non-deductible.**
7. **Pick an amount to contribute**: Multiplied by 12 for monthly funding, or select a target lump sum.
8. **Record your plan** for contribution amount, timing, and any questions you want to ask a financial advisor.

This simple worksheet or written plan helps you turn complicated rules into clear steps. By tracking your decisions, you'll have a solid plan for making the most of your IRA, whether you prefer regular savings or aiming for an annual deposit after a windfall ([5]; [4]).

KEY TAKEAWAYS

- For 2025, you can defer up to $23,500 of your own salary into a 401(k). If you're 50 or older, you can contribute an additional $7,500 as a catch-up contribution, bringing your personal maximum to $31,000. Your employer's match sits on top of these limits. These figures are adjusted periodically, so check IRS.gov each January.
- Employer matches vary widely. Some companies match dollar for dollar up to a set percentage; others match 50 cents on the dollar. Either way, the principle is the same — contribute enough to capture the full match before directing money elsewhere.
- The most expensive contribution mistake is contributing less than the match threshold. The second most expensive is stopping contributions during market downturns.
- For IRAs, the 2025 contribution limit is $7,000 ($8,000 if you're 50 or older). Whether you can deduct a Traditional IRA contribution depends on your income and whether you're covered by a workplace plan — the IRS publishes updated deductibility charts each year.
- If you get a bonus or tax refund, consider directing a portion toward your IRA before the tax deadline. You have until April 15 of the following year to make a contribution that counts for the prior tax year.

Next up: Once your money is in an account, where does it actually go? Chapter 6 breaks down your investment options without the jargon.

Chapter 6: Investing Basics: Where Does the Money Go?

Chapter at a Glance

What you´ ll learn in this chapter:

- What stocks, bonds, and mutual funds are — explained in plain language with no assumed knowledge
- What asset allocation means, and why your age and timeline should influence the mix you choose
- How target-date funds work as a hands-off option that adjusts automatically as retirement approaches
- What rebalancing is, why your portfolio drifts over time, and how to bring it back into line without stress

Estimated reading time: 20 minutes

> **FIELD NOTE** *A lot of people assume their 401(k) is "invested" and leave it there. In reality, if you never chose an investment option, your money may be sitting in a default fund that doesn't match your age, timeline, or goals. Five minutes reviewing your investment elections is one of the highest-value tasks in this book.*

When people start thinking about saving for retirement, the first question is often simple: where exactly does the money go? Many feel overwhelmed by unfamiliar terms like stocks, bonds, and funds. It can seem like a maze, especially when faced with decisions inside accounts such as 401(k)s and IRAs. Understanding how these investments work and why spreading money across different options matters is key to feeling confident and in control of your financial future.

Most of the confusion here isn't about the investments themselves — it's the jargon sitting in front of them. Strip that away and the decisions get a lot smaller and more manageable.

Retirement Investment Options Made Simple

Imagine holding a basket filled with small shares of many different businesses. This is a simple way to picture a stock fund. When people invest in stock funds through retirement accounts like 401(k)s and IRAs, they each contribute money to a big pool. The fund then uses that pool to buy pieces of many companies, often well-known names as well as smaller businesses. Through this approach, a single person does not have to pick which companies might succeed—or worry about what happens to one company's stock value—because the stock fund spreads the money across a wide group of companies. This is called diversification, and it helps reduce the chance of losing money if any one company performs poorly. The main aim of stock funds is growth. Over a long period, many companies grow in value, so the money in stock funds can increase. This makes stock funds common and attractive choices in retirement accounts, especially because people often save for retirement over many years, giving their investments time to expand and recover from short-term changes in the market [6].

Stock funds come in many types. Some focus on large, stable companies, while others include small or fast-growing firms. The mix of businesses in the fund depends on its goal. Yet, all stock funds share the idea of pooling resources and scattering investments far and wide to lower risk and raise the chance for long-term gain. For beginners, it is important to know that investing in a stock fund means not putting all your eggs in one basket. This simple idea is one reason why stock funds are the backbone of most retirement plans.

Bond funds bring a different flavor to a retirement portfolio. They are the serving of plain rice in a meal that might otherwise be too spicy. Rather than buying pieces of companies, a bond fund collects money and loans it to companies or governments. In exchange, these borrowers promise to pay back the money, along with regular interest. The interest is like steady rent for letting someone use your money. Bond funds offer a way to earn income that tends to be steadier and more predictable than what you get from stocks.

When the economy is unpredictable or stocks dip, bond funds can help keep the whole investment plan from swinging too wildly. This stability comes because companies and governments, especially strong ones, usually keep their promises to pay back bonds. By mixing in bond funds with stock funds, retirement savers are less likely to see all their hard-earned money drop during bad times in the stock market. Many 401(k) and IRA options include both stock and bond funds so that savers can find a balance between growth and safety [6].

For those seeking ease and simplicity, target date funds offer an appealing alternative. These funds work like a one-stop solution for retirement savings. The name "target date" comes from the year you plan to retire—for example, a 2055 target date fund is meant for someone retiring around 2055. The fund managers start by putting most of the money into stock funds since growth is important early on, when savers have time to wait out any market drops. As the target year gets closer, the managers shift more money toward bond funds, making the investment mix less risky and more stable. This automatic change is called "rebalancing." Investors do not need to make changes themselves because professionals do the adjusting. For beginners, this means less worry about learning when to buy or sell stock or bond funds. Picking a target date fund lets someone "set it and forget it," trusting that the fund will carefully move its money from stocks toward bonds as retirement nears [1].

Target date funds are often used as the default option in workplace retirement accounts. This is because they bring together diversification, professional management, and a slow but steady shift from growth to safety. For many savers who want to keep things simple, target date funds are a strong starting point. By teaming up with professionals who study the markets, individuals can focus on saving rather than worrying about what kind of investment mix to choose.

Each type of fund—stocks, bonds, and target date—serves a different purpose. Stock funds reach for growth but can bounce up and down. Bond funds help steady the ride and provide reliable income. Target date funds pull these ideas together and add hands-off convenience. Yet the real strength in building a retirement savings plan comes not from picking only one type, but from combining them. A foundation built on a mix of these choices can help manage risk and capture growth. The ability to blend these investments is one of the biggest benefits of both 401(k)s and IRAs, allowing beginners to build simple, strong portfolios and take their first step toward a secure retirement ([1]; [6]).

Seeing Diversity and Balance: Visuals and Metaphors

A retirement portfolio is like a carefully arranged plate at a delicious food buffet. You have already learned about stocks, bonds, and target date funds, which serve as the main ingredients. Think of stocks as spicy chili—exciting, with the potential to energize your savings, but sometimes unpredictable. Bonds are the rice or bread—steady and filling, offering stability when you need it most. Target date funds act like a well-balanced casserole, blending many tastes together and adjusting themselves as time goes by.

A typical retirement account splits across a few categories: stocks for growth, bonds for stability, maybe some cash or target-date funds depending on your timeline. None of these is meant to carry the account alone — the mix is the point.

Why does this mix matter? If you only put one dish on your tray at a lunch buffet, you miss out on flavor and nutrition. If you picked just salad and skipped everything else, you'd get full of leaves but lack protein. The same is true for investments. Putting every last dollar into just stocks might lead to a big win, or you could lose a lot if the market turns. Investing entirely in bonds keeps things calmer, but you might not keep up with rising costs over a long time. A single type of fund—even a target date fund—carries its own risks if you ignore everything else out there.

Let's see how this plays out with a simple story. Sarah, in her twenties, decides to place all her retirement savings in one new and popular stock. Co-workers praise her boldness, and at first, her investment grows rapidly. One year later, unexpected news sends the stock spiraling downward. Sarah watches her savings shrink, with no other investments to fall back on. If instead Sarah had chosen several types—some in broad index funds, some in stable bonds, and a bit in a target date fund—her pie chart would have different sections. When the stock slipped, her bonds and index funds would help cushion the loss, keeping her retirement plan steady. This combination is called diversification, and it is a simple, powerful way to protect a portfolio [3].

A beginner's portfolio might look like this: An investor in their thirties could picture their pie chart as half bright with stocks, one-quarter calm with bonds, and the rest filled in with target date funds or a little cash. A verbal chart for a more cautious investor, perhaps approaching retirement, would show less color from stocks—maybe only a quarter—while bonds and cash fill up most of the space, helping to keep things steady during market storms. These proportions help manage risk and reward. Stocks offer more growth but swing up and down; bonds and cash are less likely to drop sharply but also bring less potential gain.

Food metaphors make this easier to picture. A young investor's plate is piled high with spicy, zesty dishes—lots of stocks for growth. They can handle some heat; if one dish tastes bad, they can try another. An older saver's plate is more like comfort food—bonds are the safe, soothing mashed potatoes and soup, with just a taste of spice from a few stocks. As tastes and needs change, the plate can be rearranged, swapping out some chili for more bread and soup.

The big lesson is that no single fund or investment can do everything. Spreading your money out—like sampling different things at the buffet—means your portfolio will keep its balance, even if one part disappoints [3]. The sense of safety comes not just from picking the right dish but from having enough variety that you are never left hungry, no matter what happens.

Each investor's mix looks different. If you were to listen to this as an audio book, picture your plate changing slowly over time. In the early years, colorful slices of stocks take up more space. As retirement approaches, the pie changes shape, with stable, filling portions of bonds and cash crowding in. This gradual shift is natural and supports you as needs and tastes evolve. Guidelines and advice can help tailor the meal, making sure your portfolio stays healthy and strong throughout your journey.

By using food metaphors and visual scenes, the concepts of investment variety and diversification become clear, relatable, and much friendlier for beginners starting to build the future they want ([4]; [3]).

Practical Asset Allocation and Rebalancing Guidance

When you choose investments for your retirement account, spreading money across different investment types is only part of being prepared for the future. While picking a mix of stocks and bonds reduces the risk of one bad year destroying your savings, deciding how much of your total money should go into each investment is just as important. This is where asset allocation comes in. Asset allocation means dividing your portfolio in a way that reflects your age, your comfort with risk, and how soon you'll need the money. Think of your portfolio like building a balanced meal. Having vegetables, protein, and grains on the plate is smart, but having the right amount of each is what makes the meal healthy.

Many people start by using simple guidelines to assign the percentage each asset type will take up in their portfolio. The classic approach is the "100 minus your age" rule. Imagine Sian, who is 25. According to the rule, 100 minus 25 leaves her with 75% of her retirement savings invested in stocks, with the remaining 25% in bonds and similar safer investments. For Sian, time is on her side. Her main goal is growth, and stocks have the potential to grow more than bonds over the long run, even if the road is bumpy ([5]; [2]).

Ben, who is 45, wants to keep building wealth but also starts thinking about not losing too much if the market drops. He would put 55% of his portfolio in stocks and 45% in bonds, following the same guideline. Here, Ben's balance starts shifting: he still wants some growth from stocks, but is starting to protect what he's saved by adding more bonds. Sarah, at 65, is thinking about retirement next year. The rule gives her 35% in stocks and the rest—65%—in bonds. At this stage, Sarah's main goal is protection. She wants the steady income and stability that bonds usually provide ([5]; [2]).

Of course, this guideline is just a starting point. People live longer than when the rule was first invented, so newer recommendations like "110 minus your age" or "120 minus your age" help investors keep a bit more in stocks, especially while they're younger and looking for more growth. For example, using "120 minus your age," Sian at 25 would have a bold 95% in stocks, which suits young investors if they are comfortable with some ups and downs. If watching stocks swing up and down causes too much worry, it's fine to adjust and reduce risk. Investing, like planning a vacation, asks you to be comfortable with your plan ([5]; [2]).

Asset allocation is not a "set it and forget it" solution. As time passes and investments change in value, your mix will shift on its own. Suppose Sian's stocks do very well and grow so much that they now make up 85% of her portfolio, even though her goal was 75%. Now she's taking on more risk than she intended. Rebalancing means bringing your portfolio back to your original plan by selling a bit of what has grown faster and buying a bit more of what has lagged behind. For Sian, she could sell some stocks and buy a few more bonds until her portfolio matches her chosen mix again. This is similar to adjusting the seasoning in a recipe—just a little bit restores balance so the dish tastes right.

You don't have to make these changes by hand. Most retirement plans now offer tools that make rebalancing automatic. You can usually log into your retirement account online and select an option to rebalance your portfolio annually, quarterly, or whenever it drifts away from your chosen plan. These services do the math and the trades for you, so your portfolio keeps the right shape without constant attention [2].

Some people prefer the simplicity of target-date funds or "life-cycle" funds. These funds change your asset mix slowly as the years pass, automatically adding more bonds and lowering stocks as you get closer to retirement. For example, if you plan to retire around 2030, you might select a 2030 target-date fund. This fund will hold more stocks now and shift gradually toward bonds as 2030 nears. These funds provide a simple "hands-off" approach and are a good fit for people who want expert asset allocation without the need for ongoing decisions [2].

Whatever method you choose, the right asset allocation can give you peace of mind, knowing your investments grow for the long-term while protecting against sudden losses before retirement. Even small, regular adjustments to maintain your plan make a big difference, helping you worry less about market swings and keep your future on track ([5]; [2]).

Summary and Reflections

Now that we understand the basics of stocks, bonds, and target date funds, along with how to spread money wisely through asset allocation and rebalancing, beginners can feel confident taking their first steps toward building a secure retirement. By thinking of investments like a balanced meal or a colorful plate, it becomes easier to see why mixing different options helps protect savings while aiming for growth. Whether you choose to manage your portfolio yourself or rely on ready-made target date funds, knowing these simple concepts gives you control over your financial future without feeling overwhelmed. As you move forward, keeping these ideas in mind will help you make smarter choices, stay on track no matter what the market does, and enjoy peace of mind on your journey to a comfortable retirement.

KEY TAKEAWAYS

- Stocks represent ownership in companies and carry higher potential return with higher short-term volatility. Bonds are loans to governments or corporations that pay steady interest and carry lower risk. Most retirement portfolios hold both.
- Asset allocation is how you divide your money between stocks, bonds, and other options. A common rule of thumb: subtract your age from 110 to get an approximate percentage for stocks. A 40-year-old might hold roughly 70% stocks, 30% bonds.
- Target-date funds do the allocation work for you. They hold more stocks when you're young and gradually shift toward bonds as your target retirement year approaches. They're a solid, low-maintenance option if you'd rather not manage the mix yourself.
- Rebalancing means returning your portfolio to its intended allocation after market movements have shifted it. If stocks have grown to 85% of your portfolio when you meant to hold 70%, rebalancing brings it back. Most plans let you set this to happen automatically.
- Diversification — spreading money across many investments rather than concentrating it in a few — is the primary way to reduce the damage that any single poor performer can do to your overall account.

Next up: The tax rules, penalties, and legal exceptions that govern when and how you can access your money – and how to avoid the most expensive mistakes.

Quick Check-In

By now, you've covered some of the most important foundations of retirement planning.

If this guide is helping you feel more clear or confident about your next steps—even in a small way—consider leaving a short review once you reach the end.

Even a brief 1–2 sentence review can make a meaningful difference and help others discover this resource.

Let's keep going.

Chapter 7: Taxes, Penalties, and Loopholes: Outwitting the IRS

Chapter at a Glance

What you´ ll learn in this chapter:

- The difference between pre-tax and after-tax contributions — and how that choice determines your tax bill in retirement
- The 10% early withdrawal penalty: when it applies, and the specific exceptions that allow you to avoid it legally
- Required minimum distributions: the exact ages when they kick in, how the amounts are calculated, and the penalty for missing one
- Strategies for reducing your tax burden in retirement without crossing any lines

Estimated reading time: 22 minutes

> **FIELD NOTE** *The IRS penalty for early withdrawal isn't designed to trap you — it's designed to discourage short-term thinking about long-term money. Understanding the rules gives you real options. And knowing the legal exceptions means you're never completely locked out of your own savings if a genuine emergency arises.*

"Wait, so if I take money out early, I could lose more than I saved?" Gary asked, eyebrows raising in disbelief. Zoe nodded slowly, "Yeah, it's like the IRS waits in the shadows with a penalty net."

Pre-tax and after-tax sound like a minor technicality on a form. They're not — they decide *when* you pay the IRS, and getting that timing wrong costs real money. This chapter walks through what actually happens to your money under each choice, what the penalties are for touching it too soon, and the legal ways around them when you have no other option.

Tax Advantages—Foundations and Scenarios

Gary and Zoe are two friends starting their first real jobs. Both want to save for retirement, but "pre-tax" and "after-tax" trip them up at first. Their boss puts it simply: "Pre-tax savings shrink your taxes now. After-tax means you pay taxes before saving, but your money can come out later without more taxes."

Gary chooses a pre-tax 401(k). The money comes out of his paycheck before the IRS sees it, so if he makes $60,000 and contributes $6,000, he only pays income tax as if he made $54,000 [3]. Zoe chooses a Roth IRA. Her contribution comes from money she's already paid tax on, so her paycheck looks a little smaller today – but at retirement, none of what she withdraws gets taxed, no matter how much it's grown [4].

The trade-off is straightforward: Gary pays less tax now and more later; Zoe pays more now and nothing later. Gary's account tends to grow a little faster at the start, simply because more of his dollars are invested from day one. But every dollar he eventually withdraws gets taxed as ordinary income, at whatever his rate happens to be in retirement. Zoe's account grows more slowly out of the gate, but everything in it is already settled with the IRS – once she's past 59½ and has held the account five years, every dollar she takes out is hers, full stop.

Which one wins depends on a bet about your own future: expect a higher tax rate in retirement than you have now, and Roth usually comes out ahead. Expect a lower one, and pre-tax usually does. Nobody knows that for certain – which is exactly why a lot of people end up holding both.

Power of Tax-Deferred Growth & Withdrawal Strategies

Here's the part that doesn't get talked about enough: a tax-deferred account doesn't just delay your tax bill – it grows faster than a taxable account holding the identical investments at the identical return, because nothing gets skimmed off the top every year.

Say you invest $5,000 a year in two accounts, both earning a steady 6%. In the tax-deferred account — a 401(k) or traditional IRA — none of that 6% is taxed annually, so the full return keeps compounding. By the Rule of 72, that money doubles roughly every 12 years. In a taxable account, you owe tax each year on whatever you earned, which quietly lowers your real, compounding return — if taxes eat a quarter of your annual gains, your effective return drops closer to 4.5%, which pushes your doubling time out to about 16 years. Over 36 years, that four-year gap compounds into a meaningfully larger balance in the tax-deferred account — not because the investments were different, but because the IRS got paid later instead of every single year.

The two accounts are also taxed differently coming out. Withdrawals from a traditional 401(k) or IRA are taxed as ordinary income, at whatever rate applies in the year you take the money out [1]. Withdrawals from a Roth aren't taxed at all, because the tax was already paid going in.

This is where it pays to think ahead. Expect a higher bracket later, and new savings are usually better off in a Roth — you're locking in today's lower rate. Expect a lower bracket in retirement, and tax-deferred usually wins, since you're pushing the tax bill into a year it costs less. Most people don't actually know which bracket they'll land in decades from now, which is the real case for holding both: draw from the traditional account in your lower-income years and the Roth in your higher-income years, and you smooth out the tax bill instead of guessing once and living with it.

One caution: this only works if the money stays put until retirement. Early or unplanned withdrawals trigger the penalties covered next — so the account growing fastest on paper isn't necessarily the one to raid first.

Penalties, Pitfalls, and Workarounds

The 10% early withdrawal penalty catches most people the same way: an emergency comes up, they remember there's money sitting in a retirement account, and they pull it without checking the rules first.

The tax bill arrives a few weeks later, and it's bigger than they expected. The 10% early withdrawal penalty generally applies if you take money out before age 59½, though certain IRS-approved exceptions—such as the Rule of 55 or specific hardship circumstances—may apply. But the slap doesn't end there—income tax applies on top of the penalty, and depending on where you live, state tax can too.

The real kicker is that the penalty is calculated on top of whatever you owe in regular income tax. So, if you pull $10,000 out of your account to cover an emergency, you could lose $1,000 to the penalty right off the bat. Then, depending on your tax bracket, a few more thousand could disappear to income taxes. The 'fix' ends up leaving less cash than you started with, and the original problem is still sitting there. Emergencies don't check your birthday first, and the IRS doesn't make exceptions for honest mistakes. Medical bills, car repairs, a leaking roof, a surprise tuition bill — any of these can tempt someone to raid a retirement account without realizing what it actually costs.

Those who make it to age 59½, though, enter friendlier territory. Withdrawals are allowed for any reason, penalty-free, though the amounts are still taxed as ordinary income after years of deferment [2]. Life, however, doesn't let you sit on your savings forever. Once you reach your applicable required minimum distribution age, the government generally requires withdrawals from traditional retirement accounts. Under current law (as of 2025), required minimum distributions begin at age 73 if you were born between 1951 and 1959, or at age 75 if you were born in 1960 or later. The SECURE 2.0 Act introduced these changes, so it's worth confirming your specific RMD start age at IRS.gov or with a tax advisor. The year you turn the required age, you must begin withdrawing a set amount, calculated by dividing your account balance by a life expectancy number from an IRS chart.

These required withdrawals are not suggestions. If you forget or miss your RMD, the amount not withdrawn may be subject to an excise tax. Under current IRS rules, that tax is generally 25% of the amount not taken, and it may be reduced to 10% if the mistake is corrected in time. That makes careful RMD planning very important.

There are real exceptions, though — situations where you can tap retirement savings early without the 10% penalty, even if you still owe regular income tax. Julia, 36, faced hospital bills from emergency surgery. Her medical costs exceeded 7.5% of her adjusted gross income, so withdrawing IRA funds spared her from the 10% penalty

[2], n.d.). Another example: Mike, unexpectedly out of work, tapped his IRA to pay his family's health insurance premiums, again avoiding extra IRS charges. Then there's Paula, who, at 32, bought her first home. She pulled $10,000 from her IRA, steering clear of penalties because she hadn't owned a house in the last two years .

For parents like Ahmad, college bills brought relief—he used early withdrawals to cover his son's tuition, sidestepping a penalty. Someone thrown into disaster, like Carina after her home was leveled by a hurricane, could withdraw up to $22,000 from her account, using IRS-approved disaster relief rules. Survivors of domestic abuse or those needing urgent help may self-certify for distributions as well, with brand new rules allowing withdrawals of up to $10,000, or half their account, penalty-free [5].

Quick Reference Guide

- **Penalty Triggers:** Early withdrawal (before age 59½), except for listed exceptions.
- **Exceptions:** Medical bills over 7.5% of adjusted gross income, health insurance during unemployment, first-time home purchase (up to $10,000), qualified college expenses, disability, death, substantial disaster, certain domestic abuse, court-ordered divorce splits, and required rollovers.
- **Age Requirements:** Early withdrawal penalties generally apply before age 59½; penalty-free access generally begins after age 59½; RMDs begin at the applicable age under current law, which is 73 for many account owners and later for some younger birth cohorts.
- **Required Withdrawals:** RMDs are annual, calculated using your account balance and the applicable IRS life expectancy factor; missing an RMD may trigger an excise tax that is generally 25%, or 10% if timely corrected. To qualify for the reduced 10% rate, you must withdraw the missed amount and file IRS Form 5329 within the correction window — generally within two years of the year the RMD was due. Acting quickly is essential.

These rules are complicated, but they're not arbitrary. Once you know which exceptions apply to your situation, the penalty stops being a scary unknown and becomes a number you can actually plan around.

KEY TAKEAWAYS

- Pre-tax contributions (Traditional 401(k), Traditional IRA) reduce your tax bill now but are taxed as ordinary income when you withdraw in retirement. After-tax contributions (Roth accounts) don't give you a break today, but qualified withdrawals come out tax-free.
- The 10% early withdrawal penalty applies to most distributions taken before age 59½. There are legal exceptions, including permanent disability, certain medical expenses, first-time home purchase (Roth IRA only, up to $10,000), and separation from service at age 55 or older (401(k) only). Always verify current IRS rules before accessing funds early.
- Required minimum distributions (RMDs) are mandatory annual withdrawals from traditional retirement accounts. Under current law, RMDs begin at age 73 if you were born between 1951 and 1959, and at age 75 if you were born in 1960 or later. Missing an RMD triggers an excise tax of up to 25% of the amount not taken — reducible to 10% if corrected promptly within the IRS correction window.
- Tax-smart withdrawal strategies matter. In retirement, the order in which you draw from taxable accounts, traditional accounts, and Roth accounts can significantly reduce your total lifetime tax bill.
- Roth conversions — moving money from a Traditional to a Roth account — can be a powerful tool in lower-income years, locking in a lower tax rate on the converted amount.

Next up: How to keep your head when markets turn rocky — and why your emotional response to volatility is the biggest risk to your long-term returns.

Chapter 8: Understanding Risk: Keeping Your Cool Through Market Storms

Chapter at a Glance

What you' ll learn in this chapter:

- What investment risk actually means versus how most people emotionally experience it during a downturn
- How to identify your own risk tolerance honestly — including the behavioral habits that reveal it more accurately than any quiz
- Why panic-selling during a market drop is almost always the most expensive decision a long-term investor makes
- Practical strategies for staying calm and staying invested when financial headlines are doing their best to scare you

Estimated reading time: 20 minutes

> **FIELD NOTE** *Every market downturn has two types of investors: those who stay in and those who get out. The data on which group ends up ahead is remarkably consistent. This chapter is less about market mechanics and more about understanding your own wiring — because that's where the real risk lives.*

Every market drop produces the same split: investors who ride it out and investors who sell at the bottom and buy back in near the top. The difference between those two groups has almost nothing to do with financial knowledge. It's about what they do with their hands when they're scared.

Understanding Market Volatility and Emotional Responses

The stock market moves the same way prices move at a farm market: when more people want to buy, prices climb; when more people want to sell, they fall. The only difference is scale — millions of buyers and sellers reacting not just to what's happening right now, but to a constant stream of headlines, predictions, and economic reports [1]. A surprising election result, a disappointing product launch, a single bad earnings report — any of these can shift enough sentiment to move prices fast. That's volatility: the market processing the changing mood of millions of people at once, in real time.

The pattern underneath most bad investing decisions is simple: alarming news creates a rush of emotion, and people act on the emotion before they've thought it through. Some sell everything the moment their account dips, hoping to "stop the bleeding" — except selling during a drop doesn't protect you, it locks in the loss. Markets have a long history of recovering from downturns; the investors who come out ahead are usually the ones who did nothing while everyone around them panicked.

Other people do the opposite: they freeze. Afraid of getting it wrong, they avoid investing at all, which quietly costs them more over time than any single bad year in the market would. Both reactions — panic-selling and never starting — come from the same place: an emotional response to uncertainty, not a calculated decision.

Feeling anxious about market swings isn't a flaw; it's just human. Behavioral finance has a name for part of why: loss aversion, the well-documented tendency for losing money to hurt more than gaining the same amount feels good. That asymmetry is exactly why news stories about market drops get so much attention, and why they're so good at provoking decisions people later regret.

A few things help. Knowing why you're investing in the first place — a home, retirement, a child's education — gives you something to measure a bad week against, instead of reacting to it in isolation. So does building in a deliberate pause: when a headline spooks you, wait a day before touching anything. And it helps to remember that markets have weathered worse than whatever's in this morning's news — recessions, crashes, wars — and recovered every time.

Two people can have the exact same portfolio and very different experiences of it. One checks the app daily, reads every headline, and loses sleep over short-term dips. The other checks quarterly, shrugs off the noise, and sleeps fine. Both feel some version of fear when the market drops — the difference is what they do with it. Knowing which one you are is the real starting point for managing risk, more useful than any amount of market knowledge.

Assessing Personal Risk Tolerance and Responses to Market Drops

Most people know the feeling of watching their investment account drop and wondering whether to laugh, cry, or stick their head in the sand. Dave checks his account every time the news flashes red arrows, bracing for something scary. Mel pretends she lost her phone, just to avoid seeing any numbers. Andrew, meanwhile, refreshes his app compulsively, checking obsessively even when there's nothing new to see.These reactions all have something in common: they reveal each person's unique comfort with risk. Professional investors also react emotionally when the unexpected happens, which research shows can drive their actions even if the facts haven't changed much [2].

Knowing how much of these market "storms" you can weather is your risk tolerance. Some people are comfortable with bigger swings in exchange for higher potential growth; others would rather have a smoother, more predictable ride, even at a lower return. Neither is wrong. When the market goes down quickly, even experts sometimes shift their behavior, cutting back on risky bets—not because facts changed, but because their comfort level did [2].

Self Assessment: What's Your Risk Personality?

Let's try a simple exercise. Imagine these scenarios, read the choices, and decide which describes you best. Then see what your reaction says about the kind of investor you might be.

Scenario 1:
You open your account and see it's dropped 8% this month.
A) You immediately call a friend in a panic and consider selling everything.
B) You groan, grab coffee, and check if your plan still makes sense.
C) You shrug, put your phone down, and go outside for a walk.

Scenario 2:
A big news story reports "Markets in Turmoil."
A) You feel anxious, check all your accounts, and read dozens of

articles.
B) You skim the headlines but decide to ignore the noise unless things fall further.
C) You barely notice, maybe joke it'll make a comeback before you retire.

If you picked mostly A's:
You may have a conservative risk profile. Market drops make you nervous and reactive. You prefer knowing nothing too wild will happen to your money.

Mostly B's:
You're likely a moderate investor. Market swings bother you, but you trust in a plan. You like some growth potential but want to sleep at night.

Mostly C's:
You have an aggressive profile. You may even enjoy a little drama and see big ups and downs as part of the journey. You're aiming for higher growth and can handle the wild rides.

Understanding your profile is powerful. It lets you build a practical plan that's less likely to tempt you into panicking when headlines get scary. When you recognize your instincts, you're not fighting the market—you're working with your own emotions, which experts say is one of the key ways to reduce the risk of bad decisions during stressful times [3].

What Happens During a Market Drop?

Let's paint a quick picture. The market falls, social media explodes, and your friend texts, "Did you SEE what happened?" Now what?

- **Reaction 1:** You sell quickly, then watch anxiously as prices fluctuate. **Outcome:** You feel a jolt of relief at first, but if the market bounces back, you may regret missing out on gains.
- **Reaction 2:** You review your long-term plan, compare current losses to your goals, and decide whether to rebalance. **Outcome:** You may still feel nervous, but you stay in control using facts instead of fear.
- **Reaction 3:** You do nothing, trusting your portfolio setup. Maybe you use that energy to go for a jog or bake cookies. **Outcome:** You ride out the dip with less stress, realizing that downturns are normal and usually recover over time.

The lesson: rash moves, such as panic selling, can lock in losses and cause regret. Calm, plan-based action keeps things steady. Letting headlines drive your decisions almost always works against you.

Three Ways to Build a Portfolio

Three common approaches, depending on how much volatility you can stomach:

- **Conservative Portfolio:** Like a sturdy brick house with thick walls. Lots of bonds, cash, and only a few stocks mean fewer wild swings and steady shelter—maybe a little boring, but cozy for someone who dislikes surprises.
- **Moderate Portfolio:** Picture a well-built treehouse. A good mix of stocks and bonds gives you some excitement and gentle swaying, but it won't topple over in strong winds.
- **Aggressive Portfolio:** Think hotrod convertible on the highway. Mostly stocks, less "buffer" from bonds. You'll enjoy the wind in your hair and fast progress—but there will be potholes, and you'll feel the bumps.

Each style fits a different personality and handles market storms differently. Matching your portfolio to your comfort level cuts down on panic and helps you stay focused on your goals when things get rocky.

The next section builds on this with diversification and a long-term perspective — concrete ways to manage risk instead of just enduring it ([3]; [2]).

Long-Term Strategies for Risk Management and Resilience

Risk tolerance isn't just a personality trait to tuck away in your back pocket; it's your map for building a portfolio that doesn't crumble at the first sign of trouble. Once you know your comfort level with ups and downs, the next move is to put your money in places where storms blow but your foundation holds steady. That's where diversification and long-term thinking do their best work. Diversification just means not putting all your money in one place.

Spread it across stocks, bonds, and some cash on hand, and a bad year in one area doesn't sink the whole plan.

Market timing sounds clever in theory—who doesn't want to buy low, sell high, and look like a financial wizard? But in reality, winning that guessing game is as reliable as predicting which seagull will swipe your beach fries. Here's a classic brain-tickler: If you miss just the best 10 days in the stock market over 20 years, your total return could shrink by more than half. So picture Fred, who panics after every bad headline and jumps in and out—he ends up with a much smaller nest egg than Lola, who stretches out on a hammock and lets her investments do the work. Fred's busy worrying about the next swing; Lola just checks her balance once a year and goes back to her crossword puzzle. Time in the market, not timing the market, turns small acorns into mighty oaks [5].

Things might feel slow during quiet periods—like watching grass grow, or a dog nap through a thunderstorm. But most of your portfolio's best growth happens during the calm, boring stretches. The trick is to give your investments the patience and discipline to ride out both routine drizzle and occasional downpour.

One of the smartest ways to see if your portfolio can survive a rough patch is to run a stress test at home. Stress testing lets you look future anxiety in the eye and say, "I've got this." Here's a straightforward exercise you can use:

1. Write down the current balance of every investment account you own.
2. Imagine the market drops 20% over the next year. This might sound scary, but think of it like a weather forecast you're preparing for—not a guarantee.
3. Multiply each account balance by 0.8 (which means you're reducing the total by 20%). Record these new, lower numbers.
4. Notice which investments hurt most. Is your money mostly in stocks, which took a big dip? Or do you have bonds and cash too, which didn't drop as much?
5. Ask yourself: If this happened, could you still pay for essential goals? Would you panic, or could you stay the course?
6. Try a scenario where only tech stocks fall 25% but the rest stay flat. Adjust those values accordingly.
7. Compare your original plan and priorities to this new picture. If you don't like the answers, consider spreading things out a bit more, or lowering the risk until you sleep better at night.

Let's say you wake up, read the news, and see a big red headline: markets have tumbled. You already did your stress test. You know how things might look and where you stand. Instead of rushing to sell everything in a panic, you look over your numbers, see that your emergency fund is safe, and remind yourself that you built a mix that can handle bad weather. You spot areas that may need fixing next time you rebalance but don't feel the urge to do anything drastic right now [5].

Use a Resilience Building Checklist to make discipline a habit instead of a hope. Here's what belongs on your list:

- Check your portfolio mix once a year every January.
- Rebalance investments if a category (like stocks) drifts more than 5% from your goal.
- Set up automatic transfers—say, $50 from every paycheck to your retirement account—so investing happens whether you're busy or not.
- Keep three to six months' expenses in a separate emergency account, so you never have to sell investments at a bad time.
- Post a sticky note: "Don't panic when the market drops. Review stress test results first."
- Once a year, review your withdrawal plan to make sure it matches your life changes.
- Use check-ins, not knee-jerk changes: if the news feels scary, wait a week before making any big moves.

Treat this list as your investing fire drill. Routine checks make you quick, calm, and confident no matter what the headlines shout [4].

KEY TAKEAWAYS

- Risk in investing isn't just the chance of losing money — it's also the chance of reacting to short-term losses in ways that lock in those losses permanently. Selling during a downturn converts a paper loss into a real one.
- Your risk tolerance isn't a score on a questionnaire. It's revealed by how you actually behave when your account drops 20%. If you check it daily and feel sick, that's useful information about the allocation you can genuinely sustain.
- Markets have declined many times throughout history and have recovered every time. That doesn't mean every investment recovers, but broad, diversified portfolios across major indices have consistently done so over long enough timeframes.

- Two practical tools for staying steady: don't check your balance more than quarterly, and give yourself a personal rule that you won't make any investment changes within 72 hours of alarming financial news.
- Understanding which type of investor you resemble – the one who rides it out, or the one who acts on every headline – helps you choose a portfolio you can actually hold through a storm, rather than one that looks ideal on paper but terrifies you in practice.

Next up: The more advanced moves – rollovers, 401(k) loans, and Roth conversions – explained clearly so you can use them strategically rather than accidentally.

Chapter 9: Advanced Tactics: Rollovers, Loans, and Conversions

Chapter at a Glance

What you´ ll learn in this chapter:

- What a rollover is, why it matters when you change jobs, and the critical difference between a direct and indirect rollover
- The 60-day rule and the once-per-year IRA rollover limit — two rules that trip people up even when they're trying to do the right thing
- When borrowing from your 401(k) makes sense and when it's a trap that undermines your long-term savings
- Roth conversions: what they are, when they work in your favor, and how to approach one without a nasty tax surprise

Estimated reading time: 22 minutes

> **FIELD NOTE** *Most people encounter rollovers and Roth conversions at moments of transition — changing jobs, retiring, or getting an unexpected windfall. Those moments tend to be busy and emotional, which is exactly when financial mistakes happen. Reading this chapter before you need it is the point.*

Many people think managing retirement savings means simply putting money aside and waiting until later. However, the ways you move and use those funds can have a big impact on how well your money grows and supports you in the future. Simple actions like transferring accounts, borrowing wisely, or changing how your savings are taxed can make all the difference between missed opportunities and financial confidence.

None of these moves are complicated in isolation. What makes them risky is timing — most people only think about rollovers and conversions in the middle of a job change or a life event, which is exactly when it's easiest to make an expensive mistake.

Mastering Rollovers—Concepts, Procedures, and Common Pitfalls

A rollover lets you move your savings from one retirement account to another, such as transferring your money from a 401(k) at your old job into an IRA you open on your own. These accounts hold your money for the future, usually for retirement. A rollover helps your savings stay safe, and your money preserves important tax benefits. Imagine you switched companies and left money in your former employer's retirement plan—now, a rollover lets you keep that money growing, but possibly in a better or easier-to-manage account.

People roll over funds for several reasons. Changing jobs is one of the biggest. Whenever someone leaves an employer, the old 401(k) is typically left behind. Many people end up with small accounts scattered across several jobs. Merging everything into one account with a rollover can make financial life simpler. Sometimes, rollovers happen because a new account offers lower fees or more investment choices. Other times, people want easier access to help and guidance or to streamline paperwork and reduce the risk of forgetting about an old account.

Moving your money properly with a rollover stops you from paying unnecessary taxes and penalties. If you take money directly out of the account, the government sees it as income and taxes it. Worse, if you're not yet retirement age, you could face extra fees for early withdrawal. A rollover avoids this because the funds move from one retirement account straight into another without you touching the cash. Imagine your retirement savings as a relay baton: you want it passed swiftly from one runner to the next, never dropped or misdirected.

Visualize a side-by-side chart comparing rolling over an account to leaving it scattered or withdrawing the money. On one side, painted in green, you see tidy, combined statements and fewer passwords to remember. On the other, printed in red, you face stacks of mail, multiple websites, and lost investment opportunities. In the chart's center, you spot a warning triangle reminding you that withdrawing money from your account can trigger taxes and penalties—as if a hand reached into your piggy bank and took a chunk. In this imaginary timeline, the "green" path means more of your own money compounds for your future; the "red" path means paperwork, confusion, or abrupt losses.

Rollover Pros:

- Simplified account tracking: You only need to remember one password and get one statement.
- More investment options: IRAs, for example, give you thousands of choices.
- Lower costs: Some accounts have better fees or tools.

Rollover Cons:

- Deadlines can be strict: You may have just sixty days.
- New account fees: Sometimes the new account charges for management.
- Decision overload: More choices might feel confusing at first.

To practice, follow these steps with a real-world example. Imagine Maya leaves her job at TechHub and gets a new position at DesignWorks. Maya's old 401(k) sits untouched. She wants to combine her savings in one spot.

Checklist for Completing Your First Rollover:

1. Write down all your retirement account details. Include contact numbers, website logins, and balances.
2. Call your former employer's human resources or plan administrator. Ask for "rollover options" for your old 401(k).
3. Research the new account options—maybe an IRA at a bank or investment firm. Pick one that fits your needs.
4. Open the new account. Wait for account numbers and instructions.
5. Ask the old employer to send your savings directly to the new IRA provider. Confirm this is a direct rollover, not a cash withdrawal.
6. Fill out and submit any required paperwork. Keep copies of everything.
7. Note the date money leaves the old account and mark your calendar. Direct rollovers happen quickly, but follow up if you see delays.
8. Call the new provider to ensure the money arrived. Ask them to invest the funds as you want.
9. File all confirmation letters and statements together.

10. Review your new account online. Make sure the balance and investments are correct.

Always request a direct rollover. If Maya took a check made out to herself, not the new IRA, she might be taxed on the whole sum and lose a big chunk to penalties. That happened to Joe, who thought having cash for a week would be harmless. One mistake cost him hundreds of dollars. In another case, Hal forgot about the sixty-day limit. He meant to do everything right but waited too long; the IRS viewed it as a withdrawal, and the tax bill that followed was about as pleasant as stepping on a rake.

Stay aware of which account types you're handling—the rules can differ for Roth or traditional versions. Learning these details now will lay the foundation for more advanced topics, like borrowing from your 401(k) or converting to a Roth account, which you'll explore next and put your new skills to good use.

Understanding 401(k) Loans and Roth Conversions—When and How to Use Them

Saving efficiently for retirement often means making wise decisions about how to manage existing account balances, move money between accounts, and maximize available tools. After understanding rollovers, which help protect savings as individuals change jobs or consolidate accounts [2], it's helpful to examine two more flexible options: 401(k) loans and Roth IRA conversions. Each maneuver offers unique benefits and considerations, opening advanced paths for those who want more control, but also requiring careful steps to avoid costly pitfalls.

401(k) Loans: Accessing Retirement Funds Without Early Withdrawal Penalties

Borrowing from a 401(k) means taking out a loan from your own retirement savings, not simply withdrawing the cash. The process starts with an application through your plan administrator, who can usually provide online forms or paperwork that breaks down the amount available for borrowing. Typically, the maximum loan is either $50,000 or half your vested account balance, whichever is lower. Once approved, funds are transferred directly to your bank account, which can be a relief during emergencies such as urgent home repairs or unexpected medical bills.

Repayment works like a regular installment loan. Borrowers pay themselves back—with interest—through automatic payroll deductions, typically over a period of up to five years. The main draw is speed and ease: money is accessible without a credit check, and borrowing from yourself means the interest paid goes back into your own account. If you picture this as a simple diagram, you'd see the 401(k) account as a jar, with a small portion taken out to fix a leaking roof, then steadily refilled through each paycheck deduction.

Advantages of a 401(k) loan include fast cash availability, no impact on credit score, and a repayment plan that fits within regular income. This makes it an attractive choice for true short-term needs, like paying for temporary living expenses during a job gap or fixing plumbing before it causes major home damage. It's important to distinguish this smart use from less urgent spending: using a 401(k) loan for a fancy vacation or new gadgets can erode long-term savings and risk unnecessary penalty exposure.

The downsides are notable. Money borrowed is no longer invested, meaning it misses out on potential market gains. Missing payments, or leaving your job, can trigger plan-loan default or a plan loan offset under your plan's rules. If the outstanding balance is treated as distributed and you do not complete any available rollover by the applicable deadline, the amount may become taxable and may also be subject to the 10% early-withdrawal tax if you are under age 59½. If repayment stalls, that money doesn't just fail to go back in — it gets hit with taxes and penalties on top of that. Also, repayments are made with after-tax dollars, and withdrawn again in retirement and taxed again, raising the issue of double taxation for that loaned portion.

The key is discipline—401(k) loans may be worth considering for genuine, short-term needs with a clear ability to repay. For ongoing cash-flow problems, or as a substitute for emergency savings, these loans can quickly do more harm than good by draining retirement growth and risking penalties during financial setbacks.

Roth Conversions: Turning Pre-tax Savings Into Future Tax-free Withdrawals

A Roth conversion moves money from a traditional, pre-tax 401(k) or IRA into a Roth IRA, instantly triggering income taxes for the converted amount but promising tax-free withdrawals in retirement. For many, this strategy is a way to trade immediate taxes for later relief, especially if future tax rates are likely to be higher [4].

The mechanics are straightforward. You instruct your 401(k) or IRA provider to send all or part of your balance to a Roth IRA. On a visual level, it's like moving marbles from one clear jar, labeled "tax when withdrawn," into another, labeled "taxed now, free forever after." The key rule: any amount moved gets taxed as income that year. That makes timing essential. People nearing retirement, with unusually low income for the year—say from a job loss or a gap year—might convert some funds, stay in a lower tax bracket, and enjoy tax-free growth going forward.

Roth conversions shine for those who expect higher taxes in later years, such as professionals early in their careers or people with substantial traditional balances. Spreading conversions over multiple years—sometimes called "tax bracket laddering"—can minimize the jump into higher tax brackets. For example, suppose you typically earn $50,000 a year, putting you in a 12% income bracket. You could convert just enough each year to reach the bracket's ceiling without moving into the next bracket, maximizing after-tax dollars over several years instead of all at once.

There are disadvantages. Upfront taxes can be hefty, especially on larger balances. Roth conversions come with additional timing rules. In general, each conversion can have its own 5-year period for purposes of the early-distribution penalty, and multiple conversions can make recordkeeping and tax reporting more complicated. People close to needing their retirement savings may not benefit if they have little time for post-tax growth to compound.

For anyone considering either strategy, weighing the true cost versus future benefit is crucial. Used wisely, 401(k) loans can bridge unavoidable gaps, and Roth conversions can lock in long-term savings. Learning to choose between—and within—these options gives you valuable tools for optimizing retirement plans, with more strategies available as your understanding grows ([4]; [2]).

Tax Timing Strategies, Advanced Applications, and Real-World Examples

Many people are aware of Roth conversions but may not realize the deeper strategies that can turn this financial tool into a powerful lever for reducing lifetime taxes. Timing matters as much as the tax rate itself. Smart investors work not only to compare their current and future tax brackets, but also to choreograph conversions across multiple years to keep taxable income within the lowest possible rate. One sophisticated approach is the gradual or "laddered" conversion. Instead of converting a huge balance at once, which could push you into a much higher tax bracket, you move smaller slices over several years. Each year, you calculate how much remains until you hit the top of your current marginal bracket, converting just enough to fill that space but not spill over.

Now imagine someone named Janet who recently retired at 62. For the first time in decades, her income drops significantly, because she's drawing just a small pension and hasn't yet begun Social Security. This gap presents a golden opportunity. She can convert a chunk of her traditional IRA—maybe $30,000—while still staying within the 12% federal tax bracket. If Janet waits a few years, her Social Security and possible part-time income will push her into a higher bracket, and the conversion would cost her more in taxes. In her case, timing becomes everything.

There are times in life when income naturally falls, often unexpectedly. Layoffs, sabbaticals, or even moving to part-time work can suddenly create a lower tax year. These "income valleys" are perfect windows for conversion. Suppose David takes a year-long break between jobs. He uses the chance to convert $20,000 from his IRA, paying taxes at the lower rate for that year. Had he waited until earning his full salary again, the tax would have been almost double. Strategic timing transforms what could be just a routine transfer into real money saved.

Opportunities widen further when deductions are high. Large medical bills, charitable contributions, or casualty losses can sharply reduce your taxable income. Imagine a medical emergency leads Maria to rack up enough expenses to itemize and reduce her adjusted gross income by $20,000. That same year, she converts $25,000 from her IRA to a Roth. Thanks to her hefty deduction, her effective tax rate on that conversion is far lower than normal, making the move especially advantageous [3].

Sophisticated Roth conversion tactics also consider Required Minimum Distributions (RMDs). When pre-tax retirement funds sit untouched, the IRS eventually forces withdrawals starting at age 73, known as RMDs. These withdrawals add to taxable income and can increase Medicare premiums and taxes on Social Security benefits. By converting some assets to a Roth before RMD age, you reduce the pool of funds subject to these forced payments, gaining more control and potentially avoiding costly tax traps. Picture an imaginary chart showing two future scenarios—one where Susan never converts and is forced to take huge RMDs, facing large taxes later in life, and another where she did smaller conversions over a decade, trimming both her taxable portfolio and her future tax bill [3].

Nuanced decisions require more than gut instinct—they benefit from tested models. Modern optimization tools can simulate many future scenarios, factoring in personal details and legislative risks. For instance, Woodruff et al. [1] demonstrate how stochastic optimization helps clients decide when, how much, and in which years to convert. These tools weigh the unpredictability of tax laws and give recommendations tailored to individual circumstances. This scientific approach helps prevent overreliance on gut feelings or simple "rules of thumb" that might fail in volatile times [1].

The contrast between stories makes the lessons come alive. Shelly hears at a seminar that "Roth conversions are always great." Motivated, converts her full IRA in a record-setting bonus year, pushing a large portion of the conversion into the highest marginal tax bracket and significantly increasing her overall tax bill. Later, after taxes and unexpected job changes, she realizes the move cost her thousands more than anticipated. A checklist appears in your mind: always estimate not just your current but next year's tax bracket, check for unusual income spikes, and plan for future deductions.

For levity, picture Uncle Ed, who mistook an IRA rollover for a conversion. He ended up with taxes he hadn't even planned for and missed the chance to stretch out the process. Learning to slow down, check each move, and use tax brackets to your advantage will help ensure your Roth conversion story ends with more money in your pocket and fewer surprises down the road ([3]; [1]).

KEY TAKEAWAYS

- A rollover moves your retirement savings from one account to another without triggering taxes or penalties — as long as it's done correctly. A direct rollover (institution to institution) is the safer route. An indirect rollover hands you a check, which you must redeposit within 60 days or it becomes a taxable distribution.
- You are allowed only one IRA-to-IRA indirect rollover per 12-month period across all your IRAs combined. Exceeding this limit creates a taxable event. Direct rollovers don't carry this restriction.
- 401(k) loans can make sense in a genuine short-term bind — they're borrowed from yourself and repaid with interest that goes back to you. But if you leave your job before repaying the loan, the outstanding balance typically becomes a taxable distribution, and if you're under 59½, the 10% penalty applies.
- A Roth conversion transfers money from a Traditional to a Roth account. You pay income tax on the converted amount in the year you do it. The strategic window is a year when your taxable income is lower than usual — a gap year, early retirement, or a year with significant deductions.
- Consolidating multiple old 401(k) accounts from previous employers into a single rollover IRA simplifies management, often reduces fees, and makes it easier to apply a coherent investment strategy.

Next up: How real people in different life situations put all of this into practice — with four profiles and a step-by-step action plan you can adapt to your own circumstances.

Chapter 10: Making It Work: Real-Life Scenarios and Action Plans

Chapter at a Glance

What you´ ll learn in this chapter:

- Four real-life financial profiles — early career, mid-career, self-employed, and late starter — with specific strategies tailored to each
- How to build an emergency fund that protects your retirement savings from being raided when life goes sideways
- The danger of lifestyle creep, how it quietly erodes savings as income rises, and how to keep it in check
- Practical budgeting tools that don't require a spreadsheet degree — including zero-based budgeting and the 50/30/20 framework

Estimated reading time: 22 minutes

> **FIELD NOTE** *Abstract financial advice is easy to nod along with and do nothing about. This chapter is about specifics — real people, real numbers, real decisions. If your situation doesn't match any of the four profiles exactly, find the one closest to yours and adapt from there. The principles travel.*

Nearly half of American workers have less than $25,000 saved for retirement, and many more feel unsure about where to begin planning for their financial future. This uncertainty is not surprising, given the variety of jobs people hold, differing incomes, and how personal each journey toward retirement can be. Some are just starting their careers, while others want to catch up after years of putting off savings. Many face unique situations like self-employment without traditional retirement options. Yet, despite these differences, there is a common thread: practical steps and clear guidance can help anyone move forward with confidence. Understanding when and how to act can turn what feels like a distant goal into manageable milestones that build steadily over time.

Real-Life Retirement Scenarios and Strategies

Many people wonder how they can start preparing for retirement when their lives, finances, and even their level of knowledge about money are all so different. Some readers may have just landed their first job or paid off a bit of student debt, while others feel the pressure to make up for lost time. There are also those who run their own small businesses or freelance, who do not have a boss offering a retirement plan. No matter where readers are on this path, there are practical steps everyone can take.

Early Career Saver

Imagine Maya, 27, who started her first full-time job a year ago. She earns $45,000 a year, and retirement seems far away. At first, she is unsure if saving now is even possible with rent, groceries, and some debt. However, Maya decides to automatically move $50 from every paycheck into her workplace retirement account. Her employer also puts in an extra $30 each pay period. Maya's savings might not feel like much, but over time, these small automatic deposits—plus her employer match—will accumulate and benefit from something called compound growth.

Compound growth means the money Maya saves earns returns, and those returns then earn more returns. If she saves $100 per month and earns an average annual return of around 7%, she could accumulate approximately $250,000–$260,000 over 40 years, assuming consistent contributions and long-term market performance [6]. Starting early allows her money decades to grow, and it lowers the amount she needs to save later to reach her goals. If she ever decides to save more, even bumping up her contribution by 1% each year to match pay raises can make a surprising difference by retirement age [6].

Maya does not need to be an investment expert. By exploring simple investment options, such as "target date" retirement funds or index funds in her workplace plan, she takes reasonable risks while young—with plenty of time to ride out ups and downs in the market. Her first steps lay a solid foundation, and her confidence grows with every paycheck saved.

Mid-Career Course Correction

Sam is 46 and realizes he has saved little for retirement. He feels anxious, but wants to build momentum. He looks at his budget and chooses to cut back on smaller, less important expenses like weekly dining out. He increases his contribution to his 401(k) at work from 2% to 10% of his salary, aiming for 15% eventually—including any employer match [6].

Sam also discovers options such as opening an IRA for additional savings. He uses both step-by-step: setting up automatic contributions from each paycheck and reviewing his investments yearly. Because Sam started late, he prioritizes consistent, higher contributions and chooses investments that balance return and safety, such as a mix of stock and bond funds. Sometimes, he hesitates because the path feels steep, but remembering that every extra dollar now helps him later keeps him motivated.

He also learns about catch-up contributions. After age 50, both 401(k)s and IRAs let him contribute more each year, offering a way to accelerate savings as retirement nears. By tracking his growing balances and focusing on progress, Sam stays positive and motivated, showing that even late starters can build meaningful savings with clear steps and commitment [6].

The Self-Employed Superhero

Jamie has a freelance graphic design business and does not get a retirement plan from a boss. She learns she has choices: the Solo 401(k), SEP IRA, and a Roth IRA. She chooses a Solo 401(k), which lets her save both as "employee" and "employer," boosting her maximum tax-advantaged savings each year. In 2025, Jamie can contribute up to $70,000 if her income allows, and if her spouse helps with the business, they both benefit, allowing nearly double the savings potential [5].

Jamie likes that if her earnings vary from year to year, she can adjust her deposits. She uses a simple budget to set aside retirement contributions in high-income months and aims for consistency, even during thinner times. Compared to a traditional IRA, self-employed accounts have much higher limits. She also learns that an IRA may work in lower-income years, and the rules allow for easy setup without much paperwork.

For visual learners, imagine a chart: Solo 401(k)s allow the greatest flexibility and largest contributions for those without employees, SEP IRAs are simpler and good for lower or fluctuating incomes, and traditional/Roth IRAs are best for lower starters or as extra savings. All three let her reduce taxable income now or build up tax-free income for retirement—making these plans a strong fit for self-employed people needing adaptable solutions [5].

Each scenario highlights the need to watch for milestones and moments to reassess progress. Whether starting young, speeding up in midlife, or creating a plan as an entrepreneur, everyone benefits by pausing at key ages and goalposts to check their plan and adjust to new life changes. Continuing to review and refine savings strategies shapes a satisfying retirement journey ahead.

Milestone Timelines and Decision Points

Vivid stories often help make the steps of retirement planning feel real. Imagine Mia, just starting her teaching career at age 25, opening her first retirement account. Down the hall, Alex, in his forties, realizes he must make up for lost time after years of inconsistent savings. A few blocks away, Jamie, a self-employed graphic designer, faces unique challenges in setting up her own plan. These journeys do not unfold overnight; each unfolds through a sequence of practical milestones that bring clarity and confidence as retirement comes closer.

When beginners see retirement planning as a timeline—rather than a single event—it becomes easier to understand what needs to be done and when. Early career savers like Mia start by opening a 401(k) through work or a Roth IRA on their own. The first milestone is simple: contribute at least enough to capture any available employer match if possible. Even small payroll deductions can build a strong foundation through compound growth, where money earns interest and then that interest earns more interest over time. If Mia puts away $100 each month, she could see her savings grow substantially by her mid-thirties. By the time she is 30, she may have accumulated enough to feel secure and ready to increase her contributions, showing how initial action leads naturally to increased momentum and confidence [1].

For mid-career savers like Alex, milestones shift to periodic reviews and increases. After a promotion or raise, Alex reviews his retirement plan statement and notices his balance is not where he hoped it would be. He responds by boosting his monthly contribution from $200 to $400, helping him catch up. Another milestone occurs at age 50, when the IRS allows "catch-up" contributions. By making use of these, Alex takes advantage of rules designed to help late starters. Each adjustment—adding more after a bonus, reallocating investments as family circumstances change—marks a step forward along a personalized path [2].

The self-employed have their own journey. Jamie researches solo 401(k) plans and settles on a SIMPLE IRA that accommodates her fluctuating income. Her first milestone is picking a plan, while her next is setting up automatic transfers to make saving easier. Each year at tax time, Jamie reviews her income, adjusts her contributions, and sets aside a bit more for years when business is good. These decisions not only keep her on track but empower her to take control in a flexible way.

Several key milestones stand out as universal plot points across these narratives, no matter the starting age. The account opening marks a clear beginning. The first investment review, usually one to three years later, offers a chance to see progress and reconsider strategy. Increasing contributions—perhaps after a pay raise, an inheritance, or clearing student debt—serves as another major step. Big life events like marriage or the birth of a child often prompt a deeper review of retirement goals and account beneficiaries.

Think of your retirement plan on a timeline: account set-up, then a checkpoint at every major life event after that — a new job, a marriage, a child, a health change. Each milestone becomes a checkpoint. Reviewing accounts at age 30, 40, or 50 ensures readers catch issues before they grow. Adjusting investments—moving from stocks to bonds as retirement nears, or shifting contributions to a

Roth for tax diversity—represents a chance to steer the journey toward a desired outcome [1].

These repetitive, achievable actions also provide psychological rewards. Seeing savings rise or hitting a preset goal motivates further effort. Research shows that visualizing one's future self or breaking long-term goals into concrete steps can make people more likely to act in their best interest today, improving both motivation and follow-through [1]. These mental boosts keep savers moving forward.

As readers recognize these milestones, they can start setting individual targets. Checking investment accounts at every major birthday becomes routine. Adjusting contributions each time income changes, or after reaching a mini-goal, turns planning into a series of simple, repeatable steps. From there, it becomes second nature to track progress, reflect on choices, and seek guidance—or celebrate achievements with loved ones.

Compound growth, vesting schedules, and catch-up contributions stop being intimidating terms. Instead, they become invitations to move the story forward, one milestone at a time. Small steps today transform a distant dream into a clear, step-by-step journey that anyone can follow—no matter their starting point or background [2].

Interactive Tools for Personalized Planning

The first step in building a retirement plan is clarifying your personal vision—what makes retirement meaningful to you and how you picture day-to-day life. This is called the Goal Setting Worksheet. Start by asking yourself simple, direct questions and writing down literal answers: At what age do you want to stop working full-time? Where do you see yourself living—same city, a new country, or closer to family? Who will be with you, and how will you spend most days—volunteering, golfing, traveling, or learning something new? Once your vision is on paper, writing concrete goals anchors your plan. Begin with your target date ("I aim to retire at 65"), then set timeline-based goals ("By age 50, I want my mortgage paid off" or "Every year, I'll save $1,000 for travel expenses"). Use these to outline priorities: rank what matters most. If setbacks like inflation or rising healthcare costs happen, look for trade-offs. For example, if your priority is traveling internationally each year, estimate the total cost: two trips at $3,500 each equals $7,000 yearly just for travel. If healthcare bills unexpectedly rise, consider scaling back trips or seeking more affordable travel options to rebalance your expectations while still protecting your core plan ([4]; [3]).

Now turn to current finances by doing a Budgeting for Retirement Exercise. The goal is to identify how your existing income and expenses may free up resources for savings. First, add up your after-tax income from all sources. Next, list yearly expenses—everything from rent or mortgage and groceries to phone plans, entertainment, and subscriptions. Write these in a plain table you can easily update each year: for example, Jane earns $48,000 per year, spends $1,100 per month on rent, $350 on groceries, $200 on subscriptions, and $100 on casual takeout. Visualize each total clearly—this lets you see patterns at a glance. Jane realizes, through this process, she spends $800 annually on streaming services she barely uses. By cutting these, she redirects $800 directly into her retirement savings account. Taking it further, Jane increases her 401(k) contributions by 1% each year as her salary grows. The compounding effect means that, over a decade, these small steps could add tens of thousands in future retirement wealth [4]. Revisit your budget every year and adjust as your income, living situation, or spending habits change; adaptability protects your long-term comfort and keeps your savings rate realistic.

Investing wisely is the next foundation. Because each person's comfort with risk is different, the Investment Choice Selector connects risk tolerance with practical investment options. Think through your reactions with a short quiz: 1) If your investments lose 10% in six months, do you: a) Sell immediately to avoid more loss, b) Hold steady, or c) Buy more? 2) When you picture retirement, do you prefer stability over growth, or are you comfortable with some ups-and-downs? 3) For money you won't need for at least 10 years, do you prefer: mostly savings accounts (low risk), a mix of stocks and bonds (moderate), or mostly stocks (higher risk, more growth)? If you answered mostly a's, a conservative strategy suits you best: focus on bonds, savings accounts, and low-volatility funds. This fits those nearing retirement, prioritizing protecting what they have over chasing high returns. Mostly b's suggest a balanced mix, fitting someone in mid-career still building wealth but wary of big swings. Mostly c's match an aggressive strategy, suitable for a young worker with decades until retirement who can afford some volatility for higher potential growth. A conservative plan should expect lower, but steadier returns, while aggressive plans aim higher but carry more short-term uncertainty. Review your answers and choose investments that match both your comfort and your time horizon ([4]; [3]).

Making your plan durable means checking it regularly. The Sample Plan Review Checklist ensures you are on track and stay prepared for changes. Tick off the essentials: written goals that describe your lifestyle and priorities; a current, realistic budget with cash directed to savings; investments suited to your individual risk comfort and timelines. Two safeguards should never be skipped: after any big life change (such as a career switch or a new family member), review your plan to see if income, savings, or priorities need adjustment. Also, schedule a set calendar reminder quarterly or yearly—review your goals, savings rate, and investments, updating as your needs evolve. For example, after taking a new job with a higher salary, Maria went back to her plan mid-year, increased her savings rate, and revisited which investments matched her changed timeline and new financial goals. This routine ensures your retirement plan remains living and responsive, always moving you closer to a retirement lifestyle that feels both secure and personal ([4]; [3]).

KEY TAKEAWAYS

- There is no single retirement savings path that works for everyone. The right strategy depends on your income, age, employer benefits, self-employment status, and financial obligations — but everyone has a viable starting point.
- An emergency fund of three to six months of essential expenses is not optional — it's the thing that keeps a job loss, medical bill, or home repair from becoming an early withdrawal from your retirement account.
- Lifestyle creep is the quiet enemy of long-term savings. Every time your income rises, so does the temptation to upgrade your standard of living to match. The countermove is to direct a portion of every raise directly into your retirement savings before it enters your regular budget.
- The 50/30/20 framework — 50% to needs, 30% to wants, 20% to savings and debt — is a reasonable starting point for most people. What matters less than the exact percentages is making savings automatic so it doesn't compete with spending.
- Progress is not linear. Some years you'll save more, some years less. What determines long-term outcomes isn't perfection — it's whether you stayed in the game.

Next up: The bigger financial picture beyond retirement accounts — including HSAs, estate planning basics, and how Social Security fits into your overall plan.

Chapter 11: Beyond Retirement: Broader Money Moves for a Rich Life

Chapter at a Glance

What you' ll learn in this chapter:

- What a Health Savings Account (HSA) is — and why it functions as one of the most tax-efficient savings vehicles available
- How taxable brokerage accounts fit alongside your tax-advantaged retirement accounts as your savings grow
- The basics of estate planning: beneficiary designations, wills, and the simple steps that prevent your assets from getting tied up in probate
- How Social Security fits into the broader retirement income picture — and why the decision about when to claim it matters more than most people expect

Estimated reading time: 20 minutes

> **FIELD NOTE** *Retirement planning doesn't stop at 401(k)s and IRAs. The people who navigate retirement most comfortably tend to have thought through a few wider questions — healthcare costs, what happens to their accounts when they're gone, and whether they're leaving Social Security money on the table. This chapter covers the ones most worth your attention.*

A 401(k) and an IRA can be in perfect shape and still not protect you, if a car repair or a medical bill forces you to raid them early. The accounts in this chapter aren't retirement accounts — they're what keeps you from ever needing to touch the ones that are.

Safety Nets 101: Building and Maintaining Emergency Funds

Imagine waking up to the news that your car needs a major repair, or you've suddenly lost your job. Situations like these are unpredictable and can quickly cause stress, especially if you have no spare money set aside. An emergency fund steps in as a financial "shock absorber," protecting you from having to scramble or go into debt when life throws something unexpected your way. In its most basic form, an emergency fund is a stash of cash that covers several months' worth of essential living expenses, set aside with the single purpose of letting you pay urgent bills or get through a tough patch without touching your long-term savings like retirement funds. Having this money on hand means you do not have to tap into credit cards or investments, helping you stay on track with bigger goals while handling life's curve balls [4].

Financial experts recommend keeping enough in your emergency fund to cover three to six months of necessary expenses. Think of this as a personalized safety net. This range allows some flexibility based on your situation. If you have a steady job, reliable income, and few dependents, saving three months may feel comfortable for you. If your job is unpredictable or you're the main earner in your household, six months is usually better. This approach gives you a cushion if you lose work, face medical bills, or encounter costly home repairs, giving you space and time to recover without panic. The real value is not just the number in your bank, but the peace of mind you get from knowing you are ready for the unexpected [1].

To get started, you'll need to figure out how much you should save. Begin by listing out the expenses you must pay each month. These are your "living expenses"—the bare essentials that keep your household running. For many people, this list includes rent or mortgage, groceries, electric bills, water bills, basic transportation, insurance, and minimum payments on debts. Skip the extras like dining out, cable subscriptions, new clothes, or vacations. Add these must-have costs together to get your monthly baseline. Multiply that number by three, six, or even more, depending on how big a safety net you want or need.

The next step is deciding where to keep your emergency fund. It is crucial that you can get to this money quickly and easily, without penalty or risk of losing its value. This is why financial planners urge you to use only "liquid" accounts—accounts where your cash is always ready, like savings accounts, checking accounts, or money market accounts. Suppose your emergency fund is tied up in stocks or a long-term retirement account. In that case, you might lose money if you have to sell investments at a bad time, or you could pay penalties for early withdrawal. When your money is liquid, you gain the confidence of quick access whenever you need it. Savings accounts at a trusted bank, or money market accounts, are some of the best choices, letting you earn some interest while keeping funds available for any crisis [4].

Even if your budget feels stretched, it's okay to start with a small goal —maybe $500 or $1,000. Each payday, transfer a small amount to your emergency fund account. Automating your savings, even in tiny amounts, helps you build momentum without having to think about it. Any time you get extra cash, such as a tax refund or unexpected gift, consider moving some of it to your fund. Over time, these small steps add up. If you experience an unexpected cost, having even a small emergency buffer means you can pay the bill without derailing your long-term plans or racking up credit card debt.

Let's put this in perspective: imagine a single mother receiving an unexpected medical bill. With an emergency fund, she can cover the bill and avoid dipping into her retirement savings, preserving her future security. Or think of a young worker whose job ends suddenly. With savings equal to several months of living expenses, that person can pay rent, eat well, and look for a new job without the added burden of immediate financial crisis. The relief is as real as the dollars in the account, lowering stress and making other life plans possible [1].

An emergency fund forms the base layer of a sturdy financial safety net. Think of it as the foundation on which other protections rest. By handling shocks and everyday surprises smoothly, you gain stability. This stability, in turn, makes it easier to plan for the future and explore other tools—like specialized accounts for medical costs, insurance, or debt reduction—that build on the foundation your emergency fund sets. With this critical step in place, you prepare yourself to make decisions that strengthen your financial resilience in all areas of life.

Strategic Security: Mastering HSAs, Debt Management, and Financial Priorities

A well-built financial safety net begins with enough savings set aside for emergencies, forming a buffer that keeps unexpected bills from derailing your progress. Think of this as a cushion—a stash of cash stored in an accessible account, like a savings account at your local bank. Building up one month of basic expenses is often the first step, giving you a little breathing room. Over time, gradually increasing this buffer to cover three to twelve months lets you handle job changes, car repairs, or sudden medical bills with confidence [5].

Beyond this first line of defense, Health Savings Accounts (HSAs) offer another layer of protection. An HSA is a special account you can open if your health plan is a "high deductible health plan," or HDHP. This kind of health insurance comes with a higher deductible but lets you contribute tax-deductible dollars to your HSA. For example, imagine you sign up for an HDHP through your job. Once enrolled, you can put in money from each paycheck into the HSA—money that lowers your taxable income for the year.

The real magic of HSAs lies in something financial planners call "triple tax benefits." Imagine you put $2,000 in your HSA this year. First, that $2,000 reduces your taxable income, which may lower your tax bill—this is the first benefit. Next, the money you leave in your HSA can be invested in mutual funds or similar choices. All interest, dividends, and growth stay untaxed while the money remains in the account—this is the second benefit. The final benefit happens when you take money out of your HSA for eligible medical expenses, like prescription drugs, doctor visits, or dental work. Those withdrawals are completely tax-free. So, using an HSA to pay for a $700 prescription means you don't pay taxes on the money you earned, saved, invested, or spent—saving you quite a bit compared to using after-tax money.

With consistent yearly contributions, an HSA can become a robust healthcare fund. For instance, if you contribute $3,000 each year for a decade, invest that balance, and don't use it all right away, the account could easily grow to cover a large portion of your later-in-life medical needs. Health costs are a major part of retirement, but with an HSA, these are much less frightening. When you reach age 65, you can even use your HSA for non-medical expenses—though then you pay regular income tax, similar to how withdrawals from a traditional IRA work. This adds even more flexibility to your retirement strategy [5].

While building up savings is crucial, high-interest debt remains one of the biggest threats to financial security. Credit cards, payday loans, and some personal loans often charge interest rates that can easily soar above 20 percent. For example, if you carry a $4,000 balance on a card with 21 percent interest, you could be paying $800 or more a year just in interest. That's money better spent on savings or investments. Paying off these balances first guarantees a high return —there's no investment with a risk-free 20 percent reward.

To tackle debt, two approaches are especially popular. The "debt snowball" strategy means paying off the smallest balance first, celebrating each quick win and building momentum. Imagine you have three debts: $500, $3,000, and $10,000. By clearing the $500 loan, you gain confidence and free up a payment for the next balance. The "debt avalanche," on the other hand, attacks the highest interest rate first. If that $3,000 loan has a 25 percent rate and the $10,000 has 6 percent, the avalanche puts all extra payments toward the 25 percent debt, saving the most on interest in the long run. Both methods work, and choosing one depends on how you stay motivated to pay down debt [6].

Organizing these steps visually creates a "Financial Priorities Pyramid." Imagine the foundation as your emergency fund, topped by a layer for paying off high-interest debt. The next layer holds your HSA and other tax-advantaged accounts, with additional discretionary investing at the peak. Like building a house, a strong, wide foundation supports everything above. Funding priorities depend on your personal situation, but a simple visual might look like this: first build your emergency savings, then pay down high-interest debts, add to your HSA, and finally maximize retirement and investment accounts. These layers help direct your dollars efficiently, reducing stress and building confidence over time [5].

As your financial foundation grows sturdier, daily spending choices begin to matter even more. Thoughtful habits around budgeting and lifestyle spending gradually shift from supporting survival to shaping how you live and enjoy today, even as you continue building future security.

Smart Spending for a Rich Life: Avoiding Lifestyle Creep and Budgeting with Purpose

Imagine Marissa, who lands a modest new job after college and sets up her first apartment: a thrift-shop couch, a single mug, and a monthly budget that feels tighter than her jeans after pizza night. After her first raise, she celebrates by swapping her mug for a matching set, gets a newer couch, and treats herself to Friday takeout. A few raises later, the upgrades sneak in: dining out triples, the thrift couch becomes a sleek sectional, and "starter" TV morphs into a flatscreen that impresses the neighbors. The rent moves up, streaming subscriptions multiply, and soon, Marissa's once-lean starting budget balloons to match her paycheck. This is lifestyle creep: as income goes up, so do comforts and little luxuries, often quietly enough that it feels harmless. Yet, every new normal silently steals dollars from savings, retirement, and other important goals [2].

A "life upgrades chart" brings these choices into focus. Try picturing the journey:

- Level 1: Free coffee in the break room
- Level 2: Daily lattes from the cafe
- Level 3: Ordering trendy cold brews delivered
- Bonus Boss Level: Home espresso machine with a milk frother and a monthly subscription to rare single-origin beans

The same game plays out with tech. That "just one more" phone upgrade turns a $30 monthly bill into $80 with accessories. Streaming starts at $10, jumps to $40 with add-ons, and suddenly, it feels impossible to remember what life was like with antenna TV. The small, regular splurges might feel harmless, but they add up over time —often invisibly, as a parade of tiny pamperings parade right past savings and future goals. These little leaks in the bucket slowly erode the safety nets built with emergency funds and careful debt management, making future dreams harder to reach and leaving retirement plans shortchanged [2].

Recognizing the pattern is key. Suppose you move from brewing coffee at home for $0.20 a cup to a $4-a-day coffee shop habit. Over a year, this single "tiny splurge" quietly sucks almost $1,400 from your pocket. Or maybe you upgrade a gym membership "just because," doubling monthly costs with little extra motivation or enjoyment to show for it. Multiply that across "just a little better" apartment rent or "might as well" meal delivery, and the story is the same: the future you want drifts further away, quietly taxed by creeping comforts [3].

Everyday Budgeting Tools Made Simple

Budgeting can feel like a chore, but it doesn't have to. For beginners, zero-based budgeting makes each dollar a superhero with its own mission. If $1,800 hits your account this month, you give every dollar a job: $800 for needs, $50 for streaming shows, $40 for Friday pizza, $20 to a "rainy day" fund, and so on, until every dollar is accounted for. This way, spending gets intentional, and money does not disappear in mysterious leaks.

Percentage-based budgeting works like a flexible pie chart. Out of $2,000 a month, for the 50/30/20 method, $1,000 covers "needs" like housing and groceries, $600 goes to "wants" (dining out, entertainment), and $400 goes to savings or debt payments. Simplicity and boundaries make it feel less stressful to decide. You might see: "I've spent 85% of my wants money—time to rein in takeout." Budgeting apps now turn this tracking into a game: each expense entered nudges you up a level, sends streak notifications, or lets you do a "victory dance" GIF when you hit a goal [2].

Budgets as Joy-Drivers, Not Jailers

Budgets free you to enjoy what matters—guilt-free. Paul, for example, tried both budgeting styles: with zero-based, he allocated $25 for monthly comic books, which he loved, and with the 50/30/20 rule, he increased "fun" spending during stressful months. Flexibility means budgeting adapts with you; it is a support system, not a punishment. If an unexpected gathering or opportunity pops up, you can adjust categories while staying true to larger goals. Sustainable budgets allow for treats and spontaneity, not just discipline [3].

Find Your Spending Sweet Spot: The Values Exercise

Financial wellness peaks when money choices fit your values. Start this five-step exercise:

1. List your top money values—perhaps "security," "fun," "learning," or "experiences."
2. Rank these from most to least important.
3. Assign spending areas to each (like "family dinners" for connection or "classes" for learning).
4. Check last month's spending: label each big purchase by which value it echoes.
5. Highlight two purchases that just do not fit your priorities. Plan to change them.

For example, Sam found most spending went to food delivery for convenience—not his actual values. He shifted $50 monthly from late-night orders into painting classes, boosting both creativity and satisfaction. Here's a typical ranking:

1. Security
2. Experiences
3. Learning
4. Convenience
5. Status

Value checks help you keep the future bright and the present happy—one small swap at a time. Tiny tweaks compound to real change and joy. This values focus, layered atop budgeting and the practical foundations of emergency funds and responsible debt, creates a life that is rich in meaning and financial stability ([2]; [3]).

KEY TAKEAWAYS

- An HSA (Health Savings Account) offers a triple tax advantage: contributions are tax-deductible, growth is tax-free, and withdrawals for qualified medical expenses are tax-free. After age 65, you can withdraw for any reason and pay only ordinary income tax — making it function similarly to a Traditional IRA.
- Taxable brokerage accounts have no contribution limits and no restrictions on when you can withdraw, but gains are subject to capital gains tax. They're useful once you've maximized your tax-advantaged accounts and want to save more.
- Beneficiary designations on retirement accounts and life insurance pass outside of a will and outside of probate. This

means an outdated beneficiary designation can override your most recent wishes — review yours whenever you experience a major life change.
- Social Security replaces roughly 40% of pre-retirement income for the average worker. Claiming early (as young as 62) permanently reduces your monthly benefit; delaying past full retirement age (up to 70) permanently increases it. The decision of when to claim is one of the most consequential in retirement planning.
- A simple will and a durable power of attorney are not just for the wealthy or the elderly. They're practical documents that protect your family if something unexpected happens. An estate planning attorney can help you get both in place efficiently.

Next up: The final chapter — how to stay on track through all of life's changes and build a retirement plan that actually lasts.

Chapter 12: Winning the Long Game: Staying On Track for Life

Chapter at a Glance

What you´ ll learn in this chapter:

- How to conduct a simple annual retirement review — what to check, what to update, and how long it actually takes
- How to adapt your plan when life changes: job loss, marriage, divorce, inheritance, health shifts
- The psychology of long-term saving — the mindset habits that keep you going when motivation fades and markets test your nerve
- How to make the journey feel achievable and even enjoyable, including celebrating milestones so progress feels real

Estimated reading time: 18 minutes

> **FIELD NOTE** *The hardest part of retirement planning isn't the first step — it's year fourteen, when nothing dramatic has happened, the market has been boring, and it's easy to feel like nothing is working. The people who come out ahead are the ones who built a review habit, not those who had the most enthusiasm at the start.*

"Did you remember to check your retirement plan this year?" It's a simple question, but one many of us avoid answering. Life moves quickly—new jobs, family changes, unexpected health shifts—and it's easy to push important financial decisions to the back burner. Yet, ignoring these details can quietly unravel years of careful planning. Staying on track has less to do with expert knowledge than people assume. It's a habit — the same one, repeated on a schedule, for years that mostly feel uneventful.

Staying Flexible: Adapting and Updating Your Retirement Plans

Confidently adapting your retirement plan while life keeps changing may seem daunting, but mastering a few simple habits can make the process feel achievable for anyone. This chapter focuses on helping you stay on course for a rewarding retirement by learning to engage with your plan regularly. Life always brings surprises—whether you land a new job in another city, welcome a child or grandchild, or face sudden changes in health—so taking small, ongoing steps to adjust your path helps keep your goals within reach and your stress levels low ([3]; [4]).

Think about what happens if someone, let's call her Sandra, accepts a job offer out of state. Along with all the packing and excitement, she remembers to check whether her new employer has a retirement plan and how it fits with any old 401(k) accounts she's left behind. A quick inventory helps her spot an old account, and she decides to roll it over to her new plan, making all her investments easier to track. By acting quickly, she avoids losing track of that money and stays in control.

Another example might involve Brian and his partner, who recently welcomed a baby. They're busy, tired, and learning to parent on the fly. Yet, they still find ten minutes to update the beneficiary on their retirement account and to look at their monthly contributions. Real life rarely slows down, but these little review sessions keep their financial future on solid ground. Addressing changes as soon as they happen, instead of putting them off, saves them from scrambling later on or having to do damage control. Proactive attention like this is a solid way to keep retirement plans healthy and stress under control [3].

Taking control during uncertain times brings a real sense of empowerment. When an unexpected curveball arrives, such as a family member's illness or a shift in work responsibilities, reviewing your plans right away can help things feel less overwhelming. Rather than wait for the "perfect time," give yourself permission to respond with confidence. Many people find it helpful to set a recurring annual alert, perhaps every spring, reminding them to review their retirement accounts. This habit creates a gentle nudge to check in regularly—no elaborate spreadsheets required.

The annual review process itself is straightforward and provides a safety net against overlooked details. First, begin by gathering your latest account statements and login info. Then, walk through each account, confirming contributions, beneficiaries, and your current investment choices. Scan for forgotten assets, like old employer retirement accounts, which are easy to misplace amid life's changes. Make note of any major life updates from the past year. For example, if you bought a home, had a significant health change, or adjusted family responsibilities, consider how these might impact your risk preferences or time horizon. These checks don't need to take hours; brief, consistent attention creates peace of mind.

For absolute beginners, technology offers simple solutions. Budgeting apps such as Mint, YNAB, or even the digital dashboards from your financial provider can make it easy to see all your accounts in one place. Retirement management platforms often include reminders, calculators, and tools specifically designed for people who prefer clear guidance. The key is to use a tool that feels manageable, whether digital or just pen and paper.

A practical and approachable way to stay organized involves creating a printable milestone checklist. Posting this on your fridge, your office wall, or inside your planner serves as an everyday reminder. Example milestones include: starting or leaving a job, marriage or divorce, welcoming a child or grandchild, moving to a new home, dealing with a major health event, or receiving an inheritance. Whenever a milestone occurs, refer to your checklist to see what actions might be needed—update beneficiaries, review contributions, or check insurance coverage. The visual nature of the checklist grounds the process, turning an abstract goal into something visible for the whole family to share.

Stories highlight the impact of these strategies. For instance, Maya updates her checklist calendar each spring. She spends a single afternoon reviewing her accounts and updating her plan with her spouse. Both feel secure knowing nothing critical has slipped by unnoticed. On the other hand, Dave ignores these simple checkups. Years later, he discovers his ex-spouse is still listed as a beneficiary, and an old 401(k) remains neglected. The resulting stress could have been avoided with small, timely reviews.

Success with retirement planning often comes from motivation and ongoing learning. Staying curious and celebrating small wins—like crossing milestones off your checklist or learning something new about saving—makes the whole process more enjoyable. Not only do these habits boost your confidence, but they also provide the flexibility needed to adapt as your life evolves ([3]; [4]). Small, steady actions and a positive outlook really set you up to handle any curveball that comes your way.

Empowered Growth: Ongoing Learning and a Positive Mindset

Learning to adapt as life changes is one of the most important habits to develop for a successful retirement. Regular check-ins are a great way to spot if your retirement strategy still fits what you want and need, but real confidence grows when you keep learning about what affects your future. Even something as simple as understanding the basics—like knowing how a 401(k) differs from an IRA—can change feelings of uncertainty into a sense of empowerment. For example, some people believe a 401(k) and an IRA are nearly identical, but soon discover their unique advantages, like matching contributions with a 401(k) or the potential tax-free withdrawals of a Roth IRA. Picking up flexible budgeting techniques, perhaps by committing to save a certain percentage of income or tracking spending with a colorful chart, further supports long-term goals by turning wishful thinking into clear plans for action [1].

Embracing a mindset of lifelong learning keeps retirement planning interesting, never stale or overwhelming. Discovering not just the "what" but the "why" behind investments, tax rules, and saving strategies helps make complex topics less mysterious. Personal stories, like realizing that compound interest means earning money on your money over time, often spark excitement that fuels even more learning. Readers have celebrated milestones like figuring out compound interest by sending silly gifs to friends or treating themselves to a small luxury—making each learning step matter.

Maintaining motivation is much easier when financial education feels playful and meaningful. Humor helps break down the barrier of intimidation that so often surrounds finance. It's easy to laugh at a common mix-up, such as confusing "Roth" with "wrath," which can lighten the mood while making the term memorable. Families might invent a "Retirement Superhero" cape—maybe fashioned from an old towel or a favorite t-shirt—each time they meet a savings goal. Wearing the cape or passing it around can become a fun tradition that inspires everyone to keep moving forward.

Making Progress with Positivity

A positive outlook transforms every achievement, no matter how minor, into a reason to celebrate. Small victories, like finally understanding the difference between a "traditional" and "Roth" account, deserve the same sort of recognition as larger milestones. Someone might craft a "retirement learning trophy" out of recycled materials—perhaps a painted jar lid glued to a trophy base—or jot down a congratulatory note congratulating themselves for sticking with the learning process. These playful rituals encourage consistency and help build confidence in tackling new concepts.

Keeping curiosity active doesn't require formal classes or dense textbooks. Setting simple reminders to read a new financial article each month, subscribing to an engaging podcast hosted by someone who explains things in a straightforward way, or joining a community workshop can all provide fresh perspectives. Even picking up a pamphlet at a local library or browsing short, friendly blog posts adds up over time [2]. Making learning social, such as organizing a group chat where friends share what they've learned this week or celebrate a new budgeting trick, can spark conversations that open new paths for growth.

Visual Tools and Simple Celebrations

Visual aids make learning stick. Try creating a progress tracker filled with doodles that mark each financial milestone—a star for finishing a podcast episode, a checkmark for understanding an investment topic, or a cartoon piggy bank that gets fuller as savings goals are reached. These tools, described out loud or drawn on paper, turn progress into something you can see and share. A checklist drawn in bright colors, perhaps with a small reward written next to each step, keeps things from feeling heavy and helps you look forward to your next goal.

Rewarding yourself doesn't have to be expensive or elaborate. It might mean enjoying a cup of your favorite coffee after clarifying a confusing retirement account statement or buying a special snack when you confidently rebalance an investment allocation. The act of recognizing progress makes it much easier to keep enthusiasm high and momentum building.

Adopting curiosity and a cheerful approach to lifelong learning during retirement planning sets the stage for more than financial security. It brings more confidence, encourages a sense of achievement, and helps you navigate change with optimism and humor. These habits infuse retirement with energy and possibility, opening the door to deeper personal reflections, more creativity, and goal-setting that keeps life meaningful and vibrant at every age ([1]; [2]).

Long-Term Fulfillment: Connection, Purpose, and Your Retirement Vision

Picture this exercise as a fun way to see your retirement dreams take shape. Creating a retirement bucket list helps you discover what wakes you up with excitement and keeps you motivated beyond financial goals. The objective is to highlight what truly matters most to you, turning hopes into actions and making joy a regular part of your future. It's about finding personal meaning, not just checking boxes or filling time, and giving your retirement years purpose and direction [5].

- Think about the experiences, places, or achievements that make your heart light up. Write down everything, big or small, that you want to do, see, or learn in retirement.
- Review your brainstormed list. Circle the three items that excite you most and mean the most for your personal fulfillment.
- Select one key bucket list experience. Break it into smaller, achievable steps. If you want to take a cultural trip, research destinations and pick one, check flight and lodging options, and sketch out a simple budget.
- Add your chosen experience and action steps to your calendar, even if they're months or years away.

Imagine Gladys, recently retired, sitting at her sunny kitchen table. On her list: learn to paint, visit her friend in Portugal, and master making pasta from scratch. She circles the Portugal trip, then looks up festivals, makes a list of three affordable cities, and checks for deals online. She puts "Plan Portugal Trip" on her calendar for the weekend. Gladys sees her goal as something real—and it makes her smile every time she glances at her notes.

To reflect, ask yourself: Which bucket list idea gives me butterflies just thinking about it? How might acting on this dream change how I feel about my next chapter?

The next exercise helps you grow and protect the social connections that make life meaningful. Retirement can change your social routine —you may drift apart from work friends or find yourself missing regular interactions. The objective here is to strengthen and expand your social bonds by planning activities that put you in touch with others who share your passions. Staying socially active can lift your mood and bring a sense of belonging (*Amazon.com: Your Complete Retirement Success Collection: For Living Your Most Financially Secure and Fulfilling Future (Real Life Fun and Financial Retirement Series): 9798346609469: Press, Sage Lifestyle, Phares, Jeanne: Books*, 2025).

- List three groups or individuals you would enjoy seeing more often or connecting with in a new way.
- Write down one or two purpose-driven activities you might do with each—such as weekly walking meetups, joining a neighborhood book club, or volunteering for a charity.
- Decide when and how you'll begin. Call, text, or email to propose a date or sign up online for a group.
- Choose a spot on your calendar where you mark these social plans. Consider adding reminders so you won't forget.

For example, Sam has always liked playing chess but never had time for tournaments. He lists his local chess club, his grandkids, and neighbors who enjoy coffee. Sam decides to join the Saturday games, schedule a monthly chess match with his grandkids, and invite neighbors over for a Sunday brunch. He finds the club's contact online and sends a message about the next meetup. When Sunday rolls around, he's ready for coffee and conversation.

Prompt yourself to picture: What would a perfect social week look like for me? How would spending time with these people make each day more interesting or joyful?

The final exercise brings everything together with your personalized retirement victory plan. This is more than a checklist—it's a written, spoken, or visual declaration that celebrates your goals, tracks your progress, and adds a layer of accountability. The objective is to give your achievements the recognition they deserve, helping you celebrate small wins and build momentum for the future (*Amazon.com: Your Complete Retirement Success Collection: For Living Your Most Financially Secure and Fulfilling Future (Real Life Fun and Financial Retirement Series): 9798346609469: Press, Sage Lifestyle, Phares, Jeanne: Books*, 2025; *200+ Bucket List Ideas for Retirement - Annuity.org*, 2025).

- Think about your bucket list and new social plans. In two or three sentences, write down how you will measure your progress and celebrate each step forward.
- Choose one action to make your victory plan real. Share it with a friend or loved one, display it where you'll see it daily, or record a short audio affirmation.
- Decide how often to review your statement. Schedule a monthly calendar reminder or a special day each year to reflect and revise.

Martha writes her "Retirement Victory Statement": "Each month, I will try one new activity from my list and share photos with my family. Every season, I'll host a dinner to celebrate what I've discovered and learned." She tucks it next to the refrigerator and makes it her favorite screen saver. When friends notice her newfound energy, she shares her plan and inspires others to do the same.

Ask yourself: When I imagine achieving these goals, what am I most proud of—and how can I make sure to celebrate each win along the way?

KEY TAKEAWAYS

- Retirement planning is not a one-time task. It requires an annual check-in at minimum — reviewing contribution amounts, investment allocations, beneficiary designations, and any life changes from the past year. Most people can do this in under an hour.
- Life changes require plan changes. Marriage, divorce, a new child, a job loss, an inheritance, or a significant health event can all

affect your retirement strategy. The goal isn't to have a perfect static plan — it's to have a responsive one.

- Motivation is not a reliable fuel source over decades. Habit is. Automating your contributions, scheduling your annual review, and removing the daily decision from the equation keeps the plan running even when your enthusiasm is elsewhere.
- Celebrating milestones — your first $10,000, your first $50,000, the first year you maximized contributions — keeps the long journey feeling like a series of achievements rather than an endless march. Small recognitions build the identity of someone who manages money well.
- Retirement planning is ultimately about designing a life you'll want to live. The financial mechanics are in service of something larger — the freedom to spend time the way you choose, with the people who matter, without the shadow of financial anxiety. That's worth the effort.

Your Next Step: A Simple Way to Put This Into Action

By now, you've explored the key ideas behind building a secure and flexible retirement plan—from understanding how your accounts work to making smarter decisions about saving, investing, and withdrawals.

But knowledge is only powerful when it's put into practice.

If you'd like a simple, structured way to apply what you've learned, you can access a **free Retirement Planning Toolkit** designed to help you take the next step with clarity and confidence.

Inside the toolkit, you'll find practical resources to help you:

- Organize your retirement goals
- Track your savings and contributions
- Estimate future income and expenses
- Stay consistent with your long-term plan

These tools are designed to be straightforward and easy to use—whether you're just starting out or refining an existing plan.

You can access the toolkit here:
https://www.essentialretirementguide.com/

Alternatively, scan this QR code:

Think of it as a companion to this book—something you can return to regularly as your financial life evolves.

Small, consistent actions taken over time are what turn good intentions into real results. This toolkit is simply there to help you stay on track.

Conclusion

You started this book without a clear answer to "Traditional or Roth?" — maybe not even knowing the two were different. That gap is closed now. You know how the employer match works, why starting early beats starting big, and what happens to your money under each tax treatment: taxed now, or taxed later, never both.

None of this requires getting everything right from here on. A retirement account isn't a one-time decision — it's a habit you check in on. A few things worth circling back to as your situation changes:

- Raise your contribution percentage every time you get a raise, even by 1%.
- Review your investment mix and beneficiary designations after any major life event: a new job, a marriage, a child, a divorce.
- Rebalance once a year on a fixed schedule, not every time the market has a bad week.
- If a decision ever feels bigger than what this book covers — a large rollover, an inheritance, a business sale — that's exactly when an hour with a fee-only financial advisor pays for itself.

Thank you for spending the time on this. Most people put off learning this material for years. You didn't.

This book is intended to provide general education, not personalized financial advice.

Before You Go...

You've just completed this guide — well done on taking a meaningful step toward your financial future.

As a thank-you for reading, I've created a free bonus tool for readers — **The Retirement Readiness Scorecard**.

Scan below or click on the link to download it free and put what you've learned into action.

It takes 5 minutes and shows you exactly where you stand across 10 key areas of retirement planning.

Scan for Your Free Retirement Readiness Scorecard

Free Retirement Readiness Scorecard Download

Free Tools From Essential Retirement Guide

Five free calculators built to go alongside this series — no signup required to see your results.

Visit **essentialretirementguide.com** or scan any code below to open a tool on your phone or computer.

RMD Calculator — What's My Required Minimum Distribution?
Find out exactly how much you're required to withdraw this year, when your deadline is, and what the penalty looks like if you miss it. Based on the IRS Uniform Lifetime Table for 2026.

https://www.essentialretirementguide.com/rmd

Early Withdrawal Penalty Calculator — What Would This Really Cost Me?
See the actual dollar cost of taking money out of a 401(k) or IRA before age 59½ — penalty and tax combined. Includes seven IRS penalty exceptions including the Rule of 55 and SEPP.

https://www.essentialretirementguide.com/penalty-calc

Roth Conversion Calculator — What's My Sweet Spot?
Find the maximum you can convert from a traditional IRA to a Roth this year without pushing income into a higher tax bracket. Uses the actual 2026 IRS federal tax brackets.

https://www.essentialretirementguide.com/roth-calc

Social Security Tax Calculator — How Much of My Benefit Is Taxable?
Enter your income and filing status to see exactly how much of your Social Security benefit is subject to federal tax, based on the IRS provisional income formula.

https://www.essentialretirementguide.com/tax-calc

Social Security Claiming Age Calculator — When Should I File?
Compare your monthly benefit at age 62, your Full Retirement Age, and age 70 — and see which filing age gives you the most lifetime income based on your life expectancy.

https://www.essentialretirementguide.com/ss-calc

All tools are free to use. A personalized PDF report is available by email after you see your results.

Notes & Sources

Chapter 1: Meet Your Retirement MVPs: 401(k)s and IRAs Unveiled

1. Richmond, S. (2023, December 19). Why save for retirement in your 20s? Investopedia. https://www.investopedia.com/articles/personal-finance/040315/why-save-retirement-your-20s.asp

2. Nagpal, S. (2023, December 29). Employee Financial Literacy And Retirement Planning Behavior: A Case Study. Educational Administration: Theory and Practice. https://doi.org/10.53555/kuey.v29i4.8541

3. Thaler, R. H., & Benartzi, S. (2004, February). Save More Tomorrow: Using Behavioral Economics to Increase Employee Saving. Journal of Political Economy. https://doi.org/10.1086/380085

4. IRA vs. 401(k): What's the difference and how to choose one. (2024). Citizens. https://www.citizensbank.com/learning/ira-vs-401k.aspx

5. Roth Comparison Chart | Internal Revenue Service. (2019). Irs.gov. https://www.irs.gov/retirement-plans/roth-comparison-chart

6. The Long-term Benefits of Early Retirement Planning for Employees. (2024, November 11). SPARK. https://www.adp.com/spark/articles/2024/11/the-long-term-benefits-of-early-retirement-planning-for-employees.aspx

Chapter 2: How Money Grows: The Magic of Compound Interest

1. Harvard College. (2020). Financial literacy. Harvard College. https://college.harvard.edu/guides/financial-literacy

2. Hastings, J. S., Madrian, B. C., & Skimmyhorn, W. L. (2013, August 2). Financial Literacy, Financial Education, and Economic Outcomes. Annual Review of Economics. https://doi.org/10.1146/annurev-economics-082312-125807

3. How does compound interest work? (n.d.). Securian Financial. https://www.securian.com/insights-tools/articles/how-compound-interest-works.html

4. Fernando, J. (2024, February 28). The power of compound interest: Calculations and examples. Investopedia. https://www.investopedia.com/terms/c/compoundinterest.asp

5. Optimal Finance Daily - Financial Independence & Money Advice - Podcast | Global Player. (2014). Global Player. https://www.globalplayer.com/podcasts/42KpCG/

6. WealthWave - The Money Milestones Company - Articles for your financial knowledge and education. (2025). Wealthwave.com. https://wealthwave.com/ellenhill/blog

Chapter 3: Types of Retirement Accounts: Which One's Your BFF?

1. Folger, J. (2019). 401(k) vs. Roth IRA: What's the Difference? Investopedia. https://www.investopedia.com/ask/answers/100314/whats-difference-between-401k-and-roth-ira.asp

2. Dahle, J. M. (2025, February 16). Should I do Roth or Traditional 401(k)? The White Coat Investor. https://www.whitecoatinvestor.com/should-you-make-roth-or-traditional-401k-contributions/comment-page-2/

3. Gatti Tassin, K. (2023, August 11). A CFP poked holes in my Traditional vs. Roth strategy — does it still hold up? Money with Katie. https://moneywithkatie.com/cfp-ultimate-traditional-vs-roth-strategy

4. IRS. (2018). Types of Retirement Plans | Internal Revenue Service. Irs.gov. https://www.irs.gov/retirement-plans/plan-sponsor/types-of-retirement-plans

5. SIMPLE IRA Plan | Internal Revenue Service. (2019). Irs.gov. https://www.irs.gov/retirement-plans/plan-sponsor/simple-ira-plan

6. A Comparison of Traditional vs. Roth IRA and 401(k) Features. (2024, March 22). Mariner. https://www.marinerwealthadvisors.com/insights/a-comparison-of-traditional-vs-roth-ira-and-401k-features/

Chapter 4: Starting Strong: Opening and Funding Your Accounts

1. Whittington, K. (2023, July 13). Retirement Accounts: A Comprehensive Guide. Meld Financial. https://meldfinancial.com/saving-investing/different-types-retirement-plans/

2. 13 types of investment accounts to know | Fidelity. (2024). Fidelity.com. https://www.fidelity.com/learning-center/smart-money/investment-accounts-types

3. Caporal, J. (2021, May 26). Average Retirement Savings in the U.S.: $65,000. The Motley Fool. https://www.fool.com/research/average-retirement-savings/

4. Savings Fitness: A Guide to Your Money and Your Financial Future. (2024). DOL. https://www.dol.gov/agencies/ebsa/about-ebsa/our-activities/resource-center/publications/savings-fitness

5. Retirement Planning: Safety and Comfort in Your Golden Years. (n.d.). Annuity.org. https://www.annuity.org/retirement/planning/

6. 401(k) rules for employers: Basics, benefits & guidelines. (n.d.). Human Interest. https://humaninterest.com/learn/articles/401k-basics-for-employers/

Chapter 5: Contributions and Matching: Maximizing Every Dollar

1. Sethi, R. (2025). How does retirement work? (+ how to maximize benefits!). I Will Teach You To Be Rich. https://www.iwillteachyoutoberich.com/guide-to-retirement/

2. Loose, T. (2025, March 5). How To Max Out Your 401(k). Aol.com; AOL. https://www.aol.com/max-401-k-step-step-224243865.html

3. Choi, J. J., Haisley, E., Kurkoski, J., & Massey, C. (2017, October). Small cues change savings choices. Journal of Economic Behavior & Organization. https://doi.org/10.1016/j.jebo.2017.08.010

4. Molina, H. (2023, January 25). 7 Simple Steps to Maximize Your Retirement Savings. Lafayette Federal Credit Union. https://www.lfcu.org/news/planning-for-retirement/7-simple-steps-to-maximize-your-retirement-savings-let-us-help-you-get-on-a-path-to-a-sustainable-and-enjoyable-retirement/

5. SIMPLE IRA plan. (2019). Internal Revenue Service. https://www.irs.gov/retirement-plans/plan-sponsor/simple-ira-plan

6. Top 401(k) Pitfalls Every Moderna Employee Should Know for a Brighter Retirement. (2023). Theretirementgroup.com. https://www.theretirementgroup.com/featured-article/5448108/what-are-the-most-common-401k-mistakes-that-moderna-employees-make

Chapter 6: Investing Basics: Where Does the Money Go?

1. Horneff, V., Maurer, R., & Mitchell, O. S. (2020, May). Putting the pension back in 401(k) retirement plans: Optimal versus default deferred longevity income annuities. Journal of Banking & Finance. https://doi.org/10.1016/j.jbankfin.2020.105783

2. Chen, J. (2023, October 11). Asset Allocation. Investopedia. https://www.investopedia.com/terms/a/assetallocation.asp

3. Malik, A., & Bärbel Fürstenau. (2024, September 9). Representational visuals of abstract financial concepts: A means to foster financial literacy. Citizenship Social and Economics Education; SAGE Publishing. https://doi.org/10.1177/14788047241277768

4. APA PsycNet. (2025). Apa.org. https://psycnet.apa.org/fulltext/2015-22913-002.html

5. Wuermeling, C. (2024, November 14). Should you follow the "100 minus your age" rule? justETF. https://www.justetf.com/en/academy/100-minus-age-rule.html

6. Retiring the 401(K): A New Framework For Retirement Savings | Yale Law & Policy Review. (2020). Yalelawandpolicy.org. https://yalelawandpolicy.org/inter_alia/retiring-401k-new-framework-retirement-savings

Chapter 7: Taxes, Penalties, and Loopholes: Outwitting the IRS

1. Pinkasovitch, A. (n.d.). Retirement Savings: Tax-Deferred or Tax-Exempt? Investopedia. https://www.investopedia.com/articles/taxes/11/tax-deferred-tax-exempt.asp

2. Traditional IRA Withdrawal Rules. (n.d.). NerdWallet. https://www.nerdwallet.com/article/investing/ira-distribution-rules

3. After-tax Roth vs pretax plan contributions: Which is right for you | TIAA. (n.d.). Www.tiaa.org. https://www.tiaa.org/public/learn/retirement-planning-and-beyond/pre-tax-contributions-or-roth-after-tax-deferral

4. The Roth 403(b) After-Tax Retirement Savings Plan. (2025). Cardinal at Work; Stanford University. https://cardinalatwork.stanford.edu/benefits-rewards/resources/roth-403b-after-tax-retirement-savings-plan

5. 401(k) Withdrawals: Penalties & Rules for Cashing Out a 401(k). (2023, May 31). NerdWallet. https://www.nerdwallet.com/article/investing/early-withdrawals-401ks

Further reading:

Sandhu, J. (2025, July 4). Tax-Deferred Growth—What Is It and How Does It Work? Titan Wealth International | Wealth Management and Cross-Border Financial Services for British Expats. https://titanwealthinternational.com/learn/tax-deferred-growth/

Chapter 8: Understanding Risk: Keeping Your Cool Through Market Storms

1. Pillai, S. (2022). Behavioral finance: Understanding investor psychology in volatile markets. ShodhKosh: Journal of Visual and Performing Arts, 3(2), 1062–1073. https://doi.org/10.29121/shodhkosh.v3.i2.2022.4152

2. Huber, C., Huber, J., & Kirchler, M. (2021, July). Market Shocks and Professionals' Investment Behavior – Evidence from the

COVID-19 Crash. Journal of Banking & Finance. https://doi.org/10.1016/j.jbankfin.2021.106247

3. Kwak, E. J., & Grable, J. E. (2024, October 24). A Comparison of Financial Risk-Tolerance Assessment Methods in Predicting Subsequent Risk Tolerance and Future Portfolio Choices. Risks. https://doi.org/10.3390/risks12110170

4. Browne, E., & Sharef, E. S. (2025, June 30). Balancing Act: Building Resilient Portfolios in a Changing Landscape. Pacific Investment Management Company LLC. https://www.pimco.com/us/en/insights/balancing-act-building-resilient-portfolios-in-a-changing-landscape

5. Ways to strengthen a portfolio—especially for unpredictable markets | J.P. Morgan Private Bank U.S. (2025). Jpmorgan.com. https://privatebank.jpmorgan.com/nam/en/insights/markets-and-investing/ways-to-strengthen-a-portfolio-especially-for-unpredictable-markets

Chapter 9: Advanced Tactics: Rollovers, Loans, and Conversions

1. Woodruff, J., Haskell, W. B., & Toriello, A. (2016, August). Optimized Financial Systems Helps Customers Meet Their Personal Finance Goals with Optimization. Interfaces. https://doi.org/10.1287/inte.2016.0849

2. Rollovers of Retirement Plan and IRA Distributions | Internal Revenue Service. (n.d.). Www.irs.gov. https://www.irs.gov/retirement-plans/plan-participant-employee/rollovers-of-retirement-plan-and-ira-distributions

3. Latest Roth conversion paper - Bogleheads.org. (2024, September 5). Bogleheads.org. https://www.bogleheads.org/forum/viewtopic.php?t=438720

4. 401(k) Plan | What is a 401(k) and How Does it Work? (n.d.). Annuity.org. https://www.annuity.org/retirement/401k/

Chapter 10: Making It Work: Real-Life Scenarios and Action Plans

1. Hershfield, H. E., Goldstein, D. G., Sharpe, W. F., Fox, J., Yeykelis, L., Carstensen, L. L., & Bailenson, J. N. (2011, February). Increasing Saving Behavior Through Age-Progressed Renderings of the Future Self. Journal of Marketing Research. https://doi.org/10.1509/jmkr.48.spl.s23

2. Hershey, D. A., & Mowen, J. C. (2000, December 1). Psychological Determinants of Financial Preparedness for Retirement. The Gerontologist. https://doi.org/10.1093/geront/40.6.687

3. Kagan, J. (2019). Retirement Planning. Investopedia. https://www.investopedia.com/terms/r/retirement-planning.asp

4. Retirement Planning: Safety and Comfort in Your Golden Years. (n.d.). Annuity.org. https://www.annuity.org/retirement/planning/

5. Self-Employed Retirement Plans: Know Your Options. (n.d.). NerdWallet. https://www.nerdwallet.com/article/investing/retirement-plans-self-employed

6. Saving for retirement in your 20s and 30s | Fidelity. (n.d.). Www.fidelity.com. https://www.fidelity.com/learning-center/smart-money/retirement-savings-in-your-20s-and-30s

Chapter 11: Beyond Retirement: Broader Money Moves for a Rich Life

1. Lowrey, M. (2025, March 10). Building Financial Independence: Why an Emergency Fund Matters for Next-Generation Wealth. HBKS Wealth Advisors. https://hbkswealth.com/insights/building-financial-independence-why-an-emergency-fund-matters-for-next-generation-wealth/

2. Alabi, M. (2025, March 31). Personal Finance in the Modern World: Strategies for Saving, Investing, and Building Wealth. https://www.researchgate.net/publication/390335327_Personal_Finance_in_the_Modern_World_Strategies_for_Saving_Investing_and_Building_Wealth

3. Mohammad Shahfaraz Khan, Azad, I., Moosa, S., & Mohd Yousuf Javed. (2024, June 25). Do we really need financial literacy to access the behavioral dynamics of generation Z? A case of Oman. Heliyon; Elsevier BV. https://doi.org/10.1016/j.heliyon.2024.e32739

4. About Us - Aurora Training Advantage. (2025). Aurora Training Advantage. https://auroratrainingadvantage.com/finance/key-term/liquidity-needs-cfp/

5. Prioritizing investments - Bogleheads. (2022). Bogleheads.org. https://www.bogleheads.org/wiki/Prioritizing_investments

6. How to Plan For Your Future - Personal Finance for New Pathologists. (2021). College of American Pathologists. https://www.cap.org/member-resources/podcasts/how-to-plan-for-your-future-personal-finance-for-new-pathologists

Chapter 12: Winning the Long Game: Staying On Track for Life

1. Thames, E. W. (2018). Meet the Frugalwoods: Achieving Financial Independence Through Simple Living. Harperbusiness, An Imprint Of Harpercollinspublishers.

2. Prasad, R. (2024, November 3). 101 Ways to Smart Strategy for Successful Life Management in 2024. Medium. https://medium.com/@ratneshwarprasadsinha_66909/101-ways-to-smart-strategy-for-successful-life-management-in-2024-134240ffc1cd

3. T. Rowe Price Personal Investor - Watch: Beyond savings: Why retirement lifestyle planning is important. (2025). Troweprice.com. https://www.troweprice.com/personal-investing/resources/insights/beyond-retirement-savings-how-to-achieve-post-career-life-you-want.html

4. Wood, R. E., & Pachana, N. A. (2025, February 19). The Role of Meaning in the Retirement Transition: Scoping Review. The Gerontologist. https://doi.org/10.1093/geront/gnaf076

5. 200+ Bucket List Ideas for Retirement - Annuity.org. (2025, February 4). Annuity.org. https://www.annuity.org/retirement/lifestyle/retirement-bucket-list/

Next in The Essential Retirement Strategy Series

THE ESSENTIAL SOCIAL SECURITY RETIREMENT GUIDE

How to Maximize Your Benefits and Avoid Costly Mistakes

Social Security is one of the most important sources of income in retirement, yet many people claim benefits without fully understanding how the system works.

The Essential Social Security Retirement Guide explains how benefits are calculated, when to claim for maximum lifetime income, and how to coordinate benefits with a spouse.

Inside this upcoming guide, you'll learn how to:

- Determine the best age to claim Social Security
- Avoid common claiming mistakes that reduce lifetime benefits
- Understand spousal and survivor benefit strategies
- Plan around taxes and working during retirement

This practical guide will help you approach Social Security with confidence and build a stronger retirement income strategy.

www.ingramcontent.com/pod-product-compliance
Lightning Source LLC
LaVergne TN
LVHW021736071126
851857LV00040B/1467
9791399270402